TOUGHER THAN BULLETS

Harold Davis began his professional football career with East Fife in 1950 and was drafted for national service the following year. He was seriously injured during the Korean War and spent almost two years in recovery. He played for Rangers between 1956 and 1964, during which time he made 261 appearances in the first team and won a string of honours to earn a place in the Ibrox hall of fame. Now 78, Davis devotes much of his time to supporting the Erskine Trust.

Paul Smith is the author of numerous books on football, including *For Richer, For Poorer: Rangers – The Fight for Survival*, *To Barcelona and Beyond* and *Rangers Cult Heroes*. He is also the co-author of *Shooting Star*, the autobiography of Rangers legend Colin Stein.

TOUGHER THAN BULLETS

THE HEROIC TALE OF
A BLACK WATCH SURVIVOR
OF THE KOREAN WAR

HAROLD DAVIS
WITH PAUL SMITH

MAINSTREAM
PUBLISHING

EDINBURGH AND LONDON

First published in Great Britain in 2012 by
MAINSTREAM PUBLISHING COMPANY
(EDINBURGH) LTD
7 Albany Street
Edinburgh EH1 3UG

ISBN 9781780576183

A catalogue record for this book is available
from the British Library

Printed in Great Britain by
Clays Ltd, St Ives plc
1 3 5 7 9 10 8 6 4 2

To Vi and Alan

ACKNOWLEDGEMENTS

In a life not short of incident, I have a great many people to thank as I sit down to put the finishing touches to this book. My deepest gratitude is to those who have been beside me throughout so many of the twists and turns, particularly my wife, Vi, and son, Alan, as well as the wonderful friends who have shared the journey at various points. From my days growing up and finding my way in the world to life in the Army and the events in Korea, the adventures were shared with loyal companions. Without some of those, I would not have lived to tell my story. In football, I was equally fortunate to play alongside some of the greatest men ever to pull on the Rangers jersey – famous names that still trip off the tongue and individuals I feel privileged to be able to call teammates and friends. In more recent times, a different team was involved in bringing this book to life, and my thanks go to Paul Smith and the staff at Mainstream for their enthusiasm and encouragement.

Harold Davis

Relating a life story relies on having a tale to tell – and Harold Davis ticks every box. My thanks go to Harry for giving me the opportunity to work on this project; it was a privilege and an education. My thanks also go to Bill Campbell and the Mainstream team, including Claire Rose and Graeme Blaikie, for their efforts in bringing *Tougher Than Bullets* to fruition, as well as to Colin Macleod for his endeavours. As always, heartfelt appreciation goes to Coral, Finlay, Mia and Zara for their support, love and laughter.

Paul Smith

CONTENTS

1

A MESSAGE FROM THE FRONT LINE

I REGRET TO INFORM YOU OF REPORT RECEIVED
FROM ATTEST KURE THAT YOUR SON (22652203
CORPORAL HAROLD DAVIS, BLACKWATCH) WAS
PLACED ON THE DANGEROUSLY ILL LIST ON 22
MAY. THE ARMY COUNCIL DESIRE TO EXPRESS
THEIR SYMPATHY IN YOUR ANXIETY. LETTER
FOLLOWS SHORTLY.
                  OIC INFANTRY RECORDS, PERTH.

I CAN ONLY BEGIN TO imagine what was running through my
mother's mind when the telegram was delivered to her home in
Perth. It took fewer than 50 words to bring the news she must
have been dreading since I had been signed up for the Black
Watch and we'd set sail from British shores to head for active
service in the Korean War.

It was in May 1953 that the worst fears of those I had left
behind when I'd embarked on my adventure were realised. A slip
of paper with that brief message was all they had to go on at that
stage, with no inkling as to the events that had led to my illness.

More than 5,000 miles away, in a military hospital in Japan, I
was beginning a very different battle from the one I had been
involved in just a few weeks earlier in the barren lands of Korea.
This one was not about winning a war; it was about staying alive.

I was more determined than ever that I wouldn't be beaten.

By the time the telegram was written, I was preparing for the latest in a catalogue of operations that would save my life and repair the damage inflicted during my final night in the war zone. It had not ended the way I would have hoped and my exit from the front line was not made, ultimately, under my own steam.

The build-up to that evening had been like any other during the months I had spent in Korea. I was serving with C Company, a fantastic group that embodied all that is good about the famous Black Watch regiment.

It was during one of C Company's stints on the front line that I had come to harm. We had been rounded up and sent up to the most notorious of areas on the battleground, known quite simply as 'the Hook'. Even the name sounds menacing and it is true to say that that was quite fitting.

It was our turn to try to hold back the advances of the vicious and well-drilled Chinese and North Korean forces. It had been a horrible, stagnant war, with neither side giving a yard as the fighting was played out in and around the Hook for months and years on end.

The conflict had been raging for near enough three years by that point and there was a sense that the enemy troops were getting increasingly frustrated, desperate even, at their lack of progress. They had been pegged back, unable to claim the ground they needed to make any inroads at all. Faced with that, the signs were that they would resort to riskier and heavier attacks.

We had been shipped out and sent to a position set slightly back from the front, away on the right side of the Hook. It was a quiet section, we were told, but then we had heard that before and found ourselves sheltering from bombardments. There were no guarantees wherever you were posted, because there was no such thing as a safe place on the line, just different degrees of danger.

As a corporal, I had three gun pits to look after during the course of the night. My job was to dot from pit to pit, patrolling the position and making sure everything was in order and the team was settled and focused on the job in hand.

I took my responsibilities seriously and felt I had to be a figurehead, someone who could keep his head and think things through even when the bullets were flying and shells were dropping. It was made easier by the fact we had good men all around us, people who could be trusted to do their best in the most difficult of circumstances. And we faced plenty of those while we were out there.

This particular night, the boys were nervous, a bit jumpy. I sensed it from the moment we took over and set to work. The mood was far from ideal. I saw it as my job to calm things down and try to keep things on an even keel – but it was difficult.

What would happen was that somebody would come up with information that put the rest of the boys on edge, maybe that there had been a number of attacks in the days before, or word that we were about to prepare to move to a certain position. Anything like that would change the atmosphere and create an air of tension.

I knew all was not well, but tried to carry on as normal. I did my patrol from the top of the trench to the first pit, from where it was maybe a 40-degree angle down to the next two.

From the top to the bottom pit, there was probably a distance of no more than 60 yards. They were always designed to be spaced out enough to provide a decent spread of cover and placed at angles to give a view of all sides of the position, but they were kept close enough to keep in contact with one another and allow communication to flow easily enough. If we were attacked, the last thing you wanted was to be isolated. There would be two or three men in each pit, keeping watch and with their finger on the trigger ready to respond to any sign of danger.

Pointing out of the gaps in the pit walls were Bren guns, strong little machine guns that had been in service since the Second World War. They had a gas cylinder below the barrel that powered the rounds, and generally it was a reliable weapon. Every magazine held 30 rounds, and the guns gave us a good defence, particularly with the number we had between the three pits.

I had just checked the first pit and was doing my best to keep things upbeat; if they had sensed any sort of worry in my tone, it would only have made things worse. I remember telling the boys in that first pit, 'Look, it's a wee bit jumpy tonight, but there's nothing doing. It's all quiet out here.'

I wasn't telling a word of a lie. Despite the obvious nervousness, I hadn't seen or heard anything that I was overly worried about. As always, you could hear noises in the distance – but it was no more or less than usual. It was just the sounds of a battlefield, the clink of weapons in the darkness and the sort of thing we had all become accustomed to.

I went down to the second gun pit and knew in an instant I had a big problem. There was shouting and bawling coming from down in the darkness, a real panic going on. I could hear it long before I reached it and jumped down into the pit, roaring, 'What the f**k's going on?'

They were screaming back at me, 'We're being attacked, we're being attacked!'

They were hysterical, with real terror in their voices and etched on their faces. They believed what they were saying, there was no doubt about that, but I was desperate to try to manage the situation as best I could. If it was true, they were no use to me in the state they were in and we would all be in jeopardy.

I told them they were talking nonsense, that there was nobody around but our own men. But they were adamant that one of their Bren guns had been pulled out of the pit through its slot.

The enemy had developed a habit of stealing our weaponry whenever they could. They would creep up in the dead of night and target a single gun post, whip away the gun and make off with it. They had it down to a fine art, rarely being caught in the act and getting back to their lines to turn our own weapons on us. It solved their equipment problems and there was maybe even a sense of perverse satisfaction about killing British and other allied troops with our own bullets.

This night, my guys were convinced that it had happened to them. I kept telling them, 'You're kidding me – you're at it,' but deep down I knew it wasn't a prank. My stomach sank when they told me what had happened. It was very real and very worrying.

We had all heard about it happening elsewhere on the line and we knew the gun hadn't just vanished. For all we knew, the Chinese were still on the other side of the pit looking in at us and ready to fire. From virtually point-blank range, we'd be easy targets, and a horrible sense of dread swept over me. It wasn't panic – I still felt composed enough – but I knew we had to act and had to act fast.

If they weren't outside the pit, they must have made it back to the wire fencing that stretched along our position, adding an extra line of defence. The wire was 40 yards in front of where we were standing. If they could negotiate their way through that, they'd be back to relative safety, under the cover of darkness, and with one of our Brens in their clutches.

Neither of those two scenarios sat comfortably with me. I didn't want it happening on my watch and thought I could sort it out. As I say, a corporal's position in those situations is to patrol his gun pits and keep control of them. Here I had two of the men shouting and screaming at each other, and I'm busy saying to myself, 'It can't be happening to me – what do I do here?'

Dawn wasn't far from breaking and I was thinking to myself, 'Right, the usual time for the Chinese to make these attacks is first thing, before the light gets up. That's why everyone's in such turmoil.'

Generally speaking, you would use two out of three of your pits, but that night all three were manned because the tensions were rising. Maybe you could call it a sense of vulnerability, but whatever it was we'd felt we had to go mob-handed.

Now I was faced with a delicate wee situation. It was getting near to daylight. If they were still around our gun pits, they would have to act soon or go back through the wire before the cover of darkness was blown. There's only so much three gun pits can do if they're ambushed, but we would have to give it a go, and I had to lead from the front.

Without giving it much more than a second's thought, I climbed up over the trench top and slid down the front. All of a sudden, the safety of the pit walls was gone. I ducked down and darted towards the wire to check if it had been cut or if there was any sign of interference. I quickly swept the area in front of our position, finding nothing untoward. Panic over, perhaps.

Then it all happened. Some bastard from a position further down the line called for a flare. He'd obviously seen me moving down by the wire and wondered what was going on. Again, it came down to the stresses of the night.

As so often happened, when one flare went up another one did soon after. Then another, then another ... and so it went on. In the end, it was like daylight, with these things burning in the sky and casting a bright light over the whole patch.

I was still a good 20 yards from the trench. I started to make my way back, my pace quickening to a sprint as I found myself stuck out in the open without the cover of darkness to fall back on. I was keeping low and trying to get to the trench as fast as I could, my heart in my mouth all the time I was running back.

The next thing I knew, all hell was breaking loose. Bullets splattered all around me. As they drilled into the soft ground, the mud flew up, showering me as it kicked up from the earth and rained back down. I can remember looking up at the sky, seeing the mud teeming down against the glow being cast out by the flares and just wishing I had a switch that I could turn the lights off with.

The closer I got to our position, the more I thought I'd got away with it – but a searing pain in my foot told me different. I'd been hit. I felt a burning sensation where the bullet had gone through my boot and buried itself in my flesh. It crippled me. I fell to the ground just in front of the safety of the trench.

Then there was another flurry of bullets. It seemed like they were coming from all directions, and the noise was intense, a crackling thunder that just didn't let up. My heart was pounding; the adrenalin from being hit first time round had obviously kicked in, and I was desperate to get myself out of the firing line.

I made a dive for the trench – and got hit while I was in mid-air, so close to making it over the top to shelter. Everything had gone from breakneck pace to slow motion; I was painfully aware of what was going on all around as I launched myself towards the safety of the trench.

But I hadn't made it. That scorching sensation I had experienced just seconds before when I'd been shot in the foot had spread to the rest of my body. I knew I was in big trouble. I could feel where I'd been hit in the stomach and right across my torso. This wasn't the pain of one bullet, like I'd felt before; this was like I'd been ripped open.

I didn't scream when the bullets struck me. Hollywood has a lot to answer for, because it isn't like you see in the movies. Instead, just a single word escaped from my mouth: 'Ffffffffff . . .' You can imagine the rest. That was it, no melodramatics or grand gestures. One word, one sentiment.

I fell over the top of the trench and began to appreciate the position I was in. I could see the blood seeping through my uniform; I could feel the incredible pain from every part of my body. I had a good idea straight away that it was serious. It wasn't

17

a 'Get me out of here' one, it was more a case of 'Will I get out of here?' But never, at any stage, did I think, 'That's it, it's over.' I was saying over and over, 'Let's get through this.' All that was running through my mind was 'What on earth am I doing here?' What I knew was that if I lay down I wouldn't last five minutes. Between the blood I was losing and the fatigue after a long night on the line, there was no hope of help coming to me in time.

I struggled to my feet, managed to feel my way up the side trench and eventually stumbled towards an encampment housing one of the medical points dotted along the line. I pushed my way through the flap covering the entrance and two guys grabbed me as I fell through the doorway, starting to work on me before I'd hit the ground. I only had to look at them to know I wasn't in good shape. They weren't laughing and joking, that's for sure.

They got on the radio and I could hear them calling for a helicopter to come and get me; they needed to get me away from there and to a field hospital asap. In keeping with the events of the night so far, the evacuation plan didn't run smoothly.

We were tucked away in a position that was set in among the hills; there was nowhere for the chopper to land. They hatched an alternative plan to set down in a clearing nearby. They had to rustle up a jeep to transport me the short distance to the helicopter, with me on a stretcher on the back.

By this time, the helicopter was just about there, and I was transferred into it. It was one of the US bubble choppers, which were relatively new into service. They were put to good use out in Korea, buzzing around here, there and everywhere. For emergencies like this, they were ideal.

I was still conscious, just, at that point but perhaps not entirely lucid. The abdominal wounds were eating away at my mental and physical resistance to my condition. I can remember looking down from my resting place in the little cabin, seeing the country below me and thinking, 'Isn't that nice?'

We landed a short hop away, but far enough back from the line to be sheltered from the worst of it. I was transferred into a medical bay. That's the last thing I can remember; by that time, the morphine I'd been pumped full of at my first stop must have been working its wonders.

Five days later I came to, bandaged from the neck down to my big toe. The first things I was aware of were the tubes connecting me to machines and the bottles of medicine all around.

The most frightening thing of all wasn't looking at the bandages or wondering what lay beneath them – it was the sound, not too far away, of guns and artillery firing, and the medics muttering, 'That's those bloody Chinese at it again.'

It dawned on me then and there that we weren't that far from the line, and I knew that if they did break through and come for us they wouldn't mess about. There wouldn't be any mercy for the sick or the wounded. Just like the enemy soldier I'd seen shot before my eyes in our trenches, I was a sitting duck.

For the first time during my service in the war, I was totally defenceless, and I didn't like that feeling one bit. Up until then, no matter how futile things might have seemed in certain circumstances, it was always in my mind that I could put up a damn good fight. Even if it was me against a hundred of them, I could give it a go. Now, I had nothing to fall back on. All I could do was lie there and hope against hope that others would look after me, just as the other guys propped up in the beds around me had to do.

Back home, my nearest and dearest were unaware of the drama that was unfolding – unaware until the door went and a telegram was delivered. Then it became real for all of us.

2

A SOLDIER'S LIFE FOR ME

THE TERROR I'D EXPERIENCED ON the line in Korea was far removed from the emotions I'd felt when I'd first pulled on my British Army uniform in the more familiar surroundings of Scotland. Nobody was more proud than me to serve and nothing I experienced in war has changed my attitude towards my time in the Army. I was one of the unlucky ones in a sense, but there were others who did not make it out alive. In that regard, I can count myself fortunate.

I am also fortunate that I can count myself a Black Watch soldier. For anyone with a connection to Perth, the town where I grew up, the regiment is part and parcel of life.

When I was a schoolboy, I quickly became aware of the barracks there in the middle of town, right next to the swimming baths, and you would see the regiment training the new drafts as you went about your life on the 'outside'.

They were there to be seen, if you know what I mean, and there was a real pride in the Black Watch in Perth – indeed there still is, in what has always been an army town. Whether it was seeing the troops marching through the streets or catching a glimpse of the soldiers in the yard, there were reminders all around, and keeping the profile up was very much part of the job for those in charge.

There was a respect for the men of the regiment and for the Army as a whole, not just among us impressionable youngsters but across the board. The Second World War was not long over, and the troops were held in high esteem. They'd served with distinction and there was a certain amount of awe about what they had been through and what they had achieved.

Today, the Black Watch is still flying the flag and bearing the famous red hackle in all corners of the world. Afghanistan has been the latest port of call, and the skills the regiment is renowned for – discipline, versatility, determination and efficiency – are as relevant now as they were when I signed up in the 1950s.

Those skills may have developed and been adapted as times have changed, but the ethos has always remained the same, and much of that comes from the proud past. Everyone growing up in the area was well aware of the Black Watch and its history, particularly those of us who went to school in the years after the Second World War. Our school even shared its name with the regiment's home at Balhousie Castle. That was one of the reasons that when the call came to join I was enthusiastic about what lay ahead for me. I didn't know where it would take me or what it would lead to, but I was ready to take whatever army life threw at me.

When national service was introduced after the Second World War, opinion was divided. Some were dead against the idea; others could see the sense in making sure our forces were kept up to strength at a time when numbers were severely depleted. I think immediately after the war most felt that anything designed to keep our country safe and secure was worth supporting, but as time wore on there was a shift in some quarters.

In the end, the scheme ran from 1945 through to 1963, with boys seeing service in all corners of the world, from Germany through to Korea and Malaya, and I was among 2.5 million young men enlisted during that period. Admittedly, some were more willing than others. I was certainly among those who were quite happy to be involved and to join the cause, especially when it was my home-town regiment that I was asked to serve when the instruction eventually came through for me.

The age for being called up was 18 and I had a fair idea I would get the letter soon after my birthday. It all depended on what you were doing at the time, with some people spared national service if they were in a certain line of work or training in a particular profession. The others who missed out were those not in good enough physical shape to get through the medical, perhaps through illness, and I knew I wouldn't be in either of those categories, so my time was coming.

To be honest, I was looking forward to it; it was an exciting prospect and a whole new chapter in my life about to open. Better to go into it with that mindset than dreading what was in store. I can only imagine what it must have been like if you were feeling that way.

Conscripts take to it in different ways. Some people didn't enjoy it all, but I felt I should be there and was quite happy to join. I saw it as an opportunity to see the world and broaden my horizons, and as a chance to do something worthwhile for my country, to do my bit as so many others had done before me.

I still have nothing against the concept of national service – it is the best thing a young man can do. I would thoroughly recommend it and would gladly see it reintroduced today. When people talk about bringing it back, they often sound as if conscription would be some form of punishment, but that shouldn't be the case.

It's about instilling discipline and a sense of duty, something that would be of benefit to anyone taking part. Speaking from my own experiences, taking the rough with the smooth, I can say that being in the Army stands you in good stead for the rest of your life – whatever it may throw at you. It becomes part of who you are, gives you a real sense of identity and purpose.

Of course, you don't know that at the time. You go in with only a vague idea of what army life is all about. I turned up at the gates of the barracks with my wee letter saying the date and time to report, which had dropped through the letter box at home just a short time before. You knew what it was even before you'd opened it, with the official-looking brown envelope giving the game away.

I was pointed in the right direction, and a couple of fearsome-looking sergeants disciplined us from the first step we took inside the grounds. They bullied you about, make no mistake.

How you responded to that was an indication of how you would cope and whether you were cut out for life in the forces. Some blossomed, others wilted. One thing is for certain, it was far from an easy ride, and there was no honeymoon period. Looking back, you can see that it was all part of the test and the training, but when you're at the sharp end there's no time to analyse. All you knew was that if you stepped out of line, even a little bit, there would be hell to pay.

Of course, the strict regime led to a bit of a 'them against us' mentality between the sergeants and us new recruits. We had been thrown together as strangers but quickly developed a bond and the spirit that would see us through. Even though boys were being signed up in their droves, I didn't come across many people I knew. There was only one, a lad called Chalmers, whom I recognised from seeing him around Perth. Unfortunately, he was one of those killed in action in Korea.

At that stage, we weren't looking any further ahead than our training, concentrating on getting through that and making the best of it. We were all in the same boat. It wasn't as though any of us were volunteers, going in with a bit of muscle, thinking we were the boys. We were all young, raw and ready to become men, with a nudge – sometimes a pretty forceful one – in the right direction from the sergeants who took us under their wing.

In hindsight, it must have been a tough job for them, knocking a motley crew into shape in a short space of time. The training lasted just two and half months or so and there was a lot to pack in, starting with drills on the parade ground and building from there.

I would say that as many as three-quarters of the conscripts on national service didn't want to be there. That put them at a psychological disadvantage, which made the physical part – the marching and the training – all the harder for them. Living with the discipline was also difficult for many of the new recruits, but, having played football at a decent level with East Fife, I was used to taking orders as a sportsman, and that side of things came easily for me.

Early on at Perth, our time was spent marching, getting in step and getting our kit sorted. They were instilling a bit of discipline in all of the recruits – in any way they could. For example, they would give stupid orders that made you think, 'Christ, that's just silly,' to see if anyone would rebel. I can look back and see that was the game now, but when you're on the ground doing the work you don't see it that way. Those who didn't toe the line, who weren't team players, were soon found out, and soon found out it was better to follow orders.

We spent three weeks having the rough edges knocked off, as well as going through all the medical checks and making sure we could go the distance with the physical work.

I took to the drills and the training quickly and painlessly, and by the time we were moved out from the barracks at Perth to continue our work at Fort George, near Inverness, my spirits were high. We were sent north for the advanced part of our training, which included getting to grips with weapons and live ammunition for the first time in army uniform. It was the next stop on an adventure as far as I was concerned, something new and interesting.

We were at Fort George long enough to settle and call it home.

It was an imposing old place, not least when you were just a young boy, but it was inspiring at the same time. There was a real sense of history as you stood in the parade ground.

I will always remember our welcome to Inverness – with the mat rolled out by Sergeant Chalmers (no relation to my acquaintance from Perth) in true army style as our train pulled in at the station. He epitomised the stereotypical cruel character you expect to encounter during training in the forces. Right down to the way the toes of his boots curled up and shone like glass, he was a sight to behold and to strike fear into the heart of every man who filed onto the platform. We thought to ourselves, 'Look at this! What's in store for us here?'

There were 20 guys to each sergeant and, of course, I was in the bloody 20 that were assigned to this fearsome figure. In the end, it worked out well for me. Because he liked the way I set about our work, he took me to one side and put me on point and as the corner man for marching.

One of the things they did was an inspection of your quarters and kit. If there was anything that wasn't just perfect, they would throw it on the floor to be done again. Sometimes it was a case of any excuse to find fault.

One particular day, Sergeant Chalmers grabbed my kit and threw it straight out of the window, watching it fall to the parade ground below. I was absolutely fuming. He barked, 'Right, Davis, get down there and pick it all up.' So I did just that, all the time cursing him under my breath, and made sure I got it perfect the next time. There was no way I was going to give him reason to do that to me again, even if I didn't agree with him in the first place.

Later that day, Chalmers took me to one side and said, 'Davis, I hope you didn't take it to heart. I don't want the other guys thinking there are favourites, so I had to nail you.'

I'll never forget running out for a game at East End Park, through playing Dunfermline with Rangers, and hearing the familiar shout of 'Davis!' in a voice I'd heard a hundred times and more booming out at Fort George. It was Sergeant Chalmers, standing there in the enclosure and looking just as mean and menacing as he had done all those years earlier. He remembered me, I remembered him, and there was still the same mutual respect that we'd had back in my army days. He was hard, but, in the main, he was a fair man and he treated me well.

Even though the training was hard and unforgiving, my memories of my time in Inverness are good. After our introduction to army life in Perth, it felt as though we were building to something and every day we were growing as men and as soldiers, forming a good strong unit in the time we had together.

There was physical training and weaponry and all of that. We had to do a lot of treks, including overnight exercises. It was quite difficult, particularly for those not used to that type of stamina work. It came easily enough for me because of the football training I'd done week in and week out, and I was thankful for that when I looked around and saw some of the others flagging. It could have been a real slog if I hadn't been ready for it.

It was when you found yourself sitting on the shooting range with a gun in your hand that it began to sink in what you'd really been signed up for. It was no game – the guns were real, the bullets were real and there was the responsibility that went with that. No time for messing around, that's for sure.

I'd handled a 12-bore shotgun a few times in a hunting setting but never a rifle until I went into the army and got down to work on the range there at Fort George, spending long sessions in rain, hail or shine putting in the hours in preparation for active duty.

I picked up some shooting badges at Fort George, winning the top marksman's medal – the Crossed Rifles – to qualify among the elite. When you get one of those, it's a bit of a double-edged sword, because it means you are on call if they need someone for sniper duties. I didn't particularly fancy that line of work, and fortunately I was only called upon to do it once after I landed in Korea, which was enough as far as I was concerned.

To gain the Crossed Rifles, you had to prove your accuracy in practice, and there was only a slim margin of error. From memory, I think you couldn't miss much more than one in ten targets from distance if you wanted to earn the badge, and I came through with flying colours.

Even today, I still like to keep my eye in. To be fair, my weapon of choice these days is an air rifle rather than army-issue kit, and my targets are Scottish rather than Korean; I use my gun to give the deer a little fright when they stray into our garden and start nibbling the plants and trees. I'd never do them any harm – just a little nip on the rump to send them on their way.

I've also got a little target board set up beneath one of the trees, just to give me something to find my range when I'm leaning out of the front window. Old habits die hard! Just holding a rifle in my hands takes me back to those days at Fort George, where we had the freedom of the wide open spaces around us to go out and find our feet as soldiers.

We weren't alone, though; some of the other regiments came to stay at Fort George at that time. The Cameron Highlanders were in Inverness at the same time as us. Mind you, I always thought the Black Watch had an advantage over every other regiment in the land: we had by far the best kilt in the country.

When you see a squad of men marching in the Black Watch tartan, it is enough to send a shiver down your spine. The Gordon Highlanders and many others had nice kilts, but none came close to the Black Watch plaid. There's something about it; it looks the part. I still wear mine with immense pride, red hackle and all. Every time I pull it on, I'm reminded what it means to be part of that great regiment and to have served with so many great men. No regrets.

3

ON THE OCEAN WAVE

A BUZZ WENT ROUND THE barracks as word began to break. This was it. We were going out. The order came down that we were to prepare ourselves for active service, and we knew our destiny: the Korean War was to be our introduction to life on the battlefield.

Nerves, excitement, impatience: when you get an instruction like that, you go through every emotion as your mind races with thoughts about what lies ahead. From the moment you pull on the uniform for the first time, when you look in the mirror and realise you are on your way to becoming a soldier, you expect the day to come. When it does, though, there's nothing to prepare you for the feeling of anticipation that washes over you.

Of course, we had to get to Korea first. We began the journey by rail, travelling to England. When we were marching away from the barracks in Perth to get the train, I was ordered to be the point man, out in front of our squad of 40 men and making sure the traffic knew we were coming.

The route took us past my girlfriend's office. Vi would become my wife after the war, and I can remember her looking out of the office and waving. I wasn't able to give a wave back, knowing all too well that every move was being watched by our superiors. We were on show now, flying the flag for the Black Watch.

People would stop what they were doing, cheering us along our way. Most of us had been boys when we'd walked into the barracks for the first time, and now we were marching through the town, our town, as men.

I was out in front of a group who had become friends as well as army colleagues. From the time we went through the gate on our very first day to the time we got to the station to depart for duty in Korea, the spirit was excellent. There was never any bad feeling, no fighting and no wide guys in our company. The only people who ruled the roost were the training sergeants – exactly the way it should have been. Had there been divides or cliques, I shudder to think how it could have turned out. You need to know that everyone has one another's back.

We travelled by rail from Perth, down through Scotland and on to Liverpool. From there, we were transported to the docks to embark on a voyage that, in my case at least, led to life-changing experiences in Korea.

There was a bigger sense of friendship and togetherness once we were on the troop-ship, in even closer confines than at the barracks and with no distractions. We had only one another for company, and that's when the humour starts to come out; it's a way of easing the tension and passing the time.

The *Empire Pride* was to become my home for the weeks it took to cruise to Asia. Some of the boats taking soldiers to Korea left from Southampton and the other south-coast ports, but Liverpool marked the start of our adventure. The big white trooper loomed large on the quayside. It looked very civilised from the outside, clean and crisp and with the air of an ocean liner about it. In fact, it was a bit less glamorous than that.

It had originally been a cargo boat, built in the Clydeside yard of Barclay, Curle & Co. in 1941, before being converted to carry troops. At more than 9,000 tonnes and almost 475 feet long, the *Pride* was an imposing enough vessel and had carried soldiers as far afield as Madagascar and Sicily.

Our little trip to Korea was one of the last pieces of action the ship saw. The Government put up the 'for sale' sign in 1954 and moved her on to the Charlton Steamship Co., which in turn sold the *Pride* to the Donaldson Line. I'm told she wound up in Panama before being scrapped in Hong Kong in the 1960s.

More than half a dozen troop-ships were ferrying soldiers back and forth to Korea, all plotting a careful path through foreign waters and braving high seas and foul storms to make sure manpower was maintained.

There was no quick flight to drop us in Korea, more's the pity. Instead, we were in the cheap seats and taking the long way round, experiencing a little of what it must have been like to be a Navy seaman. I have to confess, I'm glad I chose the Army rather than a life at sea in the forces, because I'm not sure how long I would have lasted in that environment. It wasn't for me.

It's easy to look back with the rose-tinted glasses on and get all nostalgic about periods of your life, and I have to remind myself that those days and weeks on the *Pride* were far from enjoyable. Yes, there were good times and high spirits, but there were some less than enjoyable times too.

For one thing, I was seasick from virtually the first minute I set foot onboard. The bloody thing was still tied to the quay and I was suffering – not just a little bit, but seriously ill. The funny thing is that nowadays I can go out fishing on choppy waters, in a rowing boat standing on its end, and not be bothered by it, but on the ocean wave it was a different story. It was the slow roll of the big ship that got to me. I just couldn't get used to it and was like a child at Christmas when we eventually got to disembark and had solid ground beneath our feet. I never did find my sea legs.

When we saw the Bay of Biscay at its very worst and hit heavy weather in the China Sea, it was a nightmare for me and the others like me. I was sick as a dog for long, long periods of the journey and it must have weakened me.

Mind you, my predicament probably wasn't helped by the conditions below deck, where we were crammed in like sardines. There must have been ten regiments travelling with us, from England and Scotland, and thousands of men. We slept in hammocks swinging above the tables we ate at. To get out, you had to clamber over the same tables, sweaty socks and all. I'm pretty sure that wasn't the most hygienic set-up in the world, and the smell wasn't the sweetest either. I think 'industrial' would be the kindest way to describe it.

There were bright spots, of course: watching the flying fish in the Med, the amazing sunsets along the way as we ventured further and further from home. It wasn't about the purpose of the trip or the destination in itself; it was about the discoveries along the way and the experiences that were awaiting us.

The top brass tried to keep us mobile as we made our way across to Hong Kong for advanced training, but space was at a premium and there was a limit to how much physical work we could manage. It was very much a case of making do with a few laps around the deck or press-ups wherever we could find space. Really, it was a case of them finding anything for us to do to avoid leaving us lazing about in our hammocks all day, which they understandably didn't want to see. To be fair, any opportunity to stretch the legs or do a bit of training was welcomed by almost all of the men, as it broke up the day and provided a bit of variety for us.

That was the name of the game with the other training we did on the voyage across. They would scatter balloons overboard for shooting practice off the back of the boat. Not surprisingly, it was near enough impossible to hit them with the ship swaying one way and the targets bobbing another on the waves, Crossed Rifles badge or not, but at least it killed a few hours and kept our minds off the monotony of the journey.

That was one of a few distractions along the way, with an inter-regiment boxing tournament among the others. That was when I learned an important lesson: sometimes 'softly, softly' is a better approach than 'full throttle'.

All of the regiments had their own boxing team. I didn't want to get involved at all, but my sergeant said our boy needed a sparring partner and I was to be that man. I'd done a bit of boxing – something I will touch on later – and had been picked out as prime candidate to pull on the gloves.

So I followed orders and soon found our hopeful wasn't very good – I clattered him one and he ended up having to withdraw from the tournament injured. The sergeant said, 'You're the one who put him out, so you're the one taking his place.'

In the meantime, I wandered down to the other part of the ship to look at the competition – who weighed in at 25 stone and stood 6 ft 4 in. tall, built like a bull. This brute of a man, a Scottish Borderer, must have taken one look at me and thought all of his Christmases had come at once. Me? Let's just say I declared myself ill just after that and couldn't take my place in the ring. Such a shame!

In truth, the only illness I was in danger of contracting was cabin fever, but that was about to be nipped in the bud. I can remember as if it were yesterday the moment I stood on that deck and saw Hong Kong on the horizon. I thought we were near, but it was such a clear day that we'd caught sight of land from miles away and it took hours until we eventually closed in and docked.

We'd had stopovers in Egypt and Aden along the way, but arriving in Hong Kong meant we were almost at the end of the journey, and minds started to turn to the job in hand. It was almost time to go to work.

First, we had some fine tuning to attend to during a few weeks on the island. We landed in the colony during monsoon season, but it wasn't too inhospitable – a gentle acclimatisation. Nothing, however, could prepare us for the weather we were about to face in Korea.

For the time being, Ho Tung Gardens was our base, a comfortable enough home from home while we were primed for action with more weapons training – including getting to grips with the grenades that were to be part of our armoury when we hit the front line. It was all part of the learning process, although at that stage I don't imagine any of us had quite grasped just how necessary all of the training we were doing was. It's only when you're faced with enemy fire that you really understand the severity of the situation. It can't be replicated in training or illustrated by an officer standing in front of you and briefing you about what to expect.

The most basic thing we had to get used to during that stint in Hong Kong was the sensation of having live bullets flashing around our heads, which was far different from the safety of the target range. All of a sudden, it was becoming very real, and I began to realise that one false move, one little mistake, could have horrible consequences.

We were pretty much confined to base when we were out there. I've read tales of other companies and other regiments getting out to see the sights and enjoy the hospitality, with wild nights on the town, but we were rushed through the process. No letting our hair down, just hard graft. I think there had been some heavy losses just beforehand and they were desperate for reinforcements, so for us it was all work and no play. After weeks of travelling, just being able to get out and stretch our legs properly to get the lungs pumping again was a relief. As always, the training was tough but necessary.

When we were in Hong Kong, there were guys coming back

from Korea, King's Own Borderers and Argylls, and some of their stories weren't very encouraging. As I say, it was a period of particularly fierce fighting, and they didn't pull any punches or try to paint it prettier than it was when they were relaying what was happening. Nobody would have wanted them to do anything different. It was far better to be going in with our eyes open, and we were, after listening to what they had to say. The North Koreans and Chinese were a formidable fighting force, as much because of their attitude as anything else. They were, we were told, as efficient as they were brutal.

You couldn't afford to let it worry you. If you were scared to death before you set foot on Korean soil, then you were on a loser before you even got started. Instead, you had to treat it as an adventure and harness your excitement about what lay ahead. With the adrenalin pumping, it was easy to feel like you could take on the world and win.

In Charlie Company, the bulk of the men were conscripts; for some reason, they had decided not to bolster us with regulars. Perhaps they were expecting Able Company to do the business before we got involved, but that wasn't the way it panned out. The A Company lost a lot of men. They took a real hammering and we were called upon to fill the void. In truth, it felt as though there was a bit of a panic on, which didn't help to quell the nerves of some of the less enthusiastic members of the company. If they hadn't wanted to be there before they arrived in Asia, they were even less inclined to be there after realising the extent of the task we all faced. It was not going to be a walk in the park, that was for sure.

The climate had a big part to play in making it tough for all of us new faces. As we travelled by sea from Britain to Asia, we passed through warm climes, but the mercury gradually dropped the further north we travelled. It would be deep into winter by the time we finally arrived in Korea, and by then there was a biting chill in the air. Soon, conditions below deck, which had seemed horribly hot and humid, were that bit more appealing, with the warmth of the inside of the ship providing welcome shelter from the weather on the open deck. Our exposure to the elements was thankfully brief while we travelled those final stages, but our time would come.

We stopped off at Kure in Japan to be kitted out with our cold-weather gear, everything from thermal socks and thick woollen jumpers to hats, gloves and scarves. Mind you, it was basic stuff – we'd later discover that we were very much the poor relations when it came to the gear on the battlefield.

From Japan, we steamed on to our final destination, a relatively short hop to South Korea. With every passing mile, the sense of purpose was building. We were on the last lap of the warm-up and waiting for the race to start for real. Everyone handles that type of situation differently. Some went into their shell; with others, you could see a quiet, steely determination come over them; and a few tried to lighten the mood.

We landed in Pusan, as it was called then (today it's spelled Busan), on the south-eastern tip of the country. We were welcomed by a squad of Highlanders piping us off the ship and effectively into battle – a nice touch to try to calm the nerves and make us feel as much at home as was possible when we were so far from it.

There was no time for niceties, no leisurely introduction to the country that we would be fighting to defend. Instead, we were ushered straight into troop-carrying trucks for the long journey north towards the conflict zone, into the wild and open spaces beyond Seoul, to ready ourselves for battle. All the talking and all the preparation were about to stop. It was time for the real thing, time to roll the sleeves up and do our bit.

All we had to go on in terms of reports of what was happening out in the field was what had filtered back to us from fellow troops. Equally, we didn't know an awful lot about why the war was raging at all. I am far better informed now than I was back then. But I don't particularly think the knowledge I have would have had any impact if I'd had it then. When you're in the thick of things, the reasoning and the motivation for the battle is really not important. It is there to be fought, there to be won.

Back home, I think most people were happy to be settling down, in peace, after the rigours of the Second World War. The fact that there was another battle going on on the other side of the world did not make a big impression on their minds.

In fact, the Korean War had its roots in the Second World War in many ways. Korea had been something of a pawn in the Allied talks following that conflict; it was a part of the Japanese empire that was seemingly in limbo. Independence was the long-term goal, but in the meantime the Allies decided in their wisdom to split Korea in half – the north going to Russia, the south, the Republic of Korea, run by an American administration. What could possibly go wrong?

The Russians established a Stalinist regime in the North, helping local leaders to form and equip the North Korean People's Army. In the South, the US struggled to get a handle on the native political leaders, who were intent on unifying Korea.

The result of it all was a spate of border skirmishes. Then, in June 1950, the NKPA invaded the Republic. The Americans had been caught on the hop a bit, but not surprisingly didn't take kindly to the situation. They invoked the United Nations, who laid the blame firmly at the door of North Korea, and troops from across the world began to converge as a UN force. Britain leapt into action, as you'd expect, and before long the Navy was steaming towards Korea and the troops were being mustered.

Initially, it was feared the boys from the North would come down and claim Pusan as their own, but the Americans eventually managed to push them back. By the autumn of 1950, the North

Korean forces were being beaten into submission and scuttling back for cover. Unfortunately, the Chinese hadn't taken kindly to events and they sent their army in mob-handed. That was when it really got interesting, because with the extra firepower and know-how, North Korea became a far better match for South Korea and the UN force.

Over the next couple of years, talks took place and talks broke down. It became a bit of a cycle, with the main cause of dispute apparently being the future of the thousands of Communist detainees in camps operated by the South Koreans.

In the meantime, somewhere in the region of 100,000 British soldiers went out to Korea and did their bit, joining with Canadian, Australian, New Zealand and Indian units to form the 1st Commonwealth Division.

More than 1,000 British men never returned, killed in action. I was among more than 2,000 who were wounded, while around half that number are said to have been posted missing or taken prisoner during the conflict. The American Department of Defense acknowledged that almost 40,000 of its servicemen died, either in battle or of other causes, while estimates on the number of South Koreans killed run as high as 137,000. The other side? They didn't do too well either. It's been suggested in some quarters that more than 400,000 Chinese troops were killed and that the North Koreans lost 215,000 – big figures, and an indication of the scale of the war. The truth is we're unlikely ever to have a totally accurate picture from the North, as there was a cloak of secrecy around the scale of the enemy's death toll.

Eventually, peace did break out, in July 1953, when agreement was reached on the prisoners. Those who wanted to go back to the North were allowed to do so; those who did not were granted asylum in the South. Prisoners of war from both sides were exchanged as part of the deal brokered to end the war, and a demilitarised zone was set up along the length of the border.

The official armistice was signed on 27 July – three years and a month after the war had broken out. It was a sudden end to the fighting, by all accounts unexpected and, although welcome, a shock to the troops who were still out there. It had taken more than two years of negotiations to get to that point, with the battles continuing and lives being lost all the time.

Even after the war had ended, the military presence was still high in the South. The Australians remained in place for years as observers, while America has always retained a presence, clearly wary of a repeat of the conflict. In the North, the battered and demoralised army retreated to lick their wounds and regroup. UN peacekeeping missions were a relatively new concept at the time, the first one having been carried out in the Middle East in 1948, but UN forces came into their own as a border patrol in Korea from 1953. The old 'blue helmets' stayed there until the 1960s to maintain the ceasefire.

Late in 1966, the North Koreans were back to their old tricks, ramping up attacks on UN troops, specifically Americans, on the border. For a couple of years, the fighting kicked off again and carried on in the same brutal way but on a smaller scale than we had experienced. This time, the North Koreans eventually pared back their attacks and the uneasy truce was resumed in 1969. South Korea remained free, the goal all along, and could continue along the path of becoming an established modern nation. I remember sitting watching the Seoul Olympics in 1988 and marvelling at what had become of the country, and feeling the same during the World Cup in 2002. Contrast that with the footage you see coming out of North Korea and you realise it could all have been very different.

4

WELCOME TO THE FRONT LINE

IT WAS COLD, IT WAS damp and it was gloomy. As we snaked our way through the Korean countryside, it wasn't what you might have expected when you first discovered you were being posted to deepest Asia. In fact, there were more than a few echoes of Scotland around us as we adjusted to our new surroundings, from the less than exotic weather to some familiar-looking terrain.

After making our way north from Pusan, we trundled into the camp where the rest of the regiment was stationed and dragged our travel-weary bodies out of the trucks to begin to explore the base that would become familiar in the weeks and months ahead. There were no frills, but there was a sense of community.

Alpha Company had taken a hell of a beating in the days before we arrived and had been pulled out of the line to regroup, taking respite in the big tents that peppered the area. We joined them there in the camp and, despite their troubles and the casualties they had suffered, we were made to feel welcome, and there was no sense that morale was at rock bottom. There was still everything to play for, to borrow a football phrase.

It was Christmas-time and we had arrived just in time for turkey and the rest of the goodies being dished up by the sergeants – although it has to be said they didn't look too happy about having to serve the squaddies. They did, though, and we lapped it up.

It was all good fun, and the little welcome reception carried on into the small hours in the main big tent at the heart of the camp. Still, all the time there were jeeps standing by with their engines revved up, ready for emergencies. You were never far from a reminder that it was a battle zone that you were in now, not a holiday camp.

After everything we had been through in training and on our way to Korea, this was the start of the proper work. We were surrounded by the more industrial trappings of war, and it began to sink in that we weren't far now from being involved in the heavy-duty action. The waiting wasn't enjoyable; once you were there, you wanted to get started and put to use the skills you had been learning.

Just a couple of days after we arrived, about a dozen of the new recruits and I were herded into a truck and we found ourselves heading towards the front line. We hadn't had long to get our bearings, but we all knew what lay in the direction we were travelling in. This was it; this was our time.

It was a dark, cold and inhospitable night. Even the quiet seemed threatening somehow, as we were left alone with our thoughts. It was a short journey in terms of distance, but it felt like it took an eternity.

We were dumped close to Charlie Company's position and found a corporal waiting to take us up to the gun pits in groups of three. In the black of the night, we climbed up a steep hill and made our way along a ridge towards the line, feeling our way as we got used to the soft conditions underfoot.

The corporal guiding us told us to keep quiet and watch our step. He had barely got the words out of his mouth when there was a terrific explosion. The three of us rookies hit the ground, scrambling for cover and hoping the world wasn't about to fall in on us. The noise was deafening and we were struck down with terror – until the corporal shouted, 'Get up, you stupid buggers, that's our own mortars that are firing!' Fortunately, it was dark and nobody could see our blushes. As far as we had been concerned, we were coming under attack. After all, we hadn't heard serious fire before, only what we'd experienced in the rather more cosseted and protected environment of the ranges at home and in Hong Kong.

You could call it beginners' nerves. Before long, I'm sorry to say, the sound of shelling and gunfire became part of everyday life and you carried on your daily business totally unperturbed by the mayhem that was going on all around you. When you were down on the line, the toilets were open-air affairs that lined a section of the trench. You'd sit with your back to the wall, knowing the action was all going on over your shoulder, and, quite often, you'd watch as shells sailed over your head and landed within sight of where you were sitting. It's fair to say laxatives weren't required, not least if one of the explosives landed a little too close for comfort!

That night with the false alarm was our first taste of the front line, albeit a quiet part of the line. In time, we would discover that there were far more perilous places to be in and around our territory, and we had clearly been given what our superiors considered a relatively gentle introduction to our new life. I like to think there was thought put into every aspect of the way the battle was won; it certainly felt like that at the time. There was a sense of purpose and of organisation that gave you faith in what we were trying to accomplish and belief that it could be done.

After our little initiation ceremony at the hands of our mortar-wielding gunners, the rest of the new drafts and I were split up and sent one by one into separate hooches – the word we used for living quarters out on the line. A hooch sounds almost quaint. In fact, I should explain, there wasn't too much cosy or comfortable about them. Nor was there much warmth in the welcome I received when I shuffled into the den allocated to me.

For as long as I live, I will never forget that night, my first on the line. I pulled back the blanket hanging at the entrance to 'my' hooch and found a single candle lighting the room, that and the faint glow from the smouldering embers burning in an old weapons drum. A real fire was not allowed, nor was smoke, for fear of drawing attention from the enemy. The slightest sign of light in the dark would see the Chinese and North Koreans throw everything in your direction. Anyone breaking that little edict would find there'd be hell to pay. Orders were followed to the letter; discipline was absolutely paramount and everyone recognised that. The rules were there for our own protection, after all.

Huddled around the drum with their hoods up were three men, looking like the witches from *Macbeth* in the near dark. Not one of them so much as glanced up from the embers they were watching so intently; not one uttered a word. I didn't feel particularly welcome. The nearest they got to conversation was a grunt.

In an instant, the reality of war struck home. After the relative high spirits of the voyage across and the nervous energy of the camp after our arrival, this was the business end of life in the army – and it didn't look like a barrel of laughs, even on this 'quiet' part of the line.

To describe the accommodation as basic would be an understatement. The hooches varied in size, but the design was roughly the same. Cut out into the ground and with walls built up from sandbags, they had two sets of two-tier bunks on two of the walls. The bunks were made from metal bedposts with old telephone wire stretched across to create a makeshift base. They weren't made for a good night's sleep, but then you never really relaxed when you were out on the front. Everyone had to sleep battle-ready, with full kit on and weapons to hand, so even with your eyes closed you never switched off. That half-asleep state became so familiar, your body refused to give in and let you close down completely. It was almost as though a special mechanism had kicked in to keep you alert and ready to deal with danger. Of course, that would catch up with you over time, but in the moment it felt entirely natural.

After my underwhelming introduction to life on the line, I settled in for the first night not really knowing what lay in store or what would be expected of me. Just before dawn, I got my answer when we were called from our bunks and mustered at the forward trench. Most of the enemy attacks were coming early in the morning, at first light, and the command was to be ready for them.

When we passed the guys in the mortar pit, it was difficult to miss the smirks. They obviously knew they'd put the fear of death into us the night before with their little performance – a case of 'Welcome to the front line, new boys'.

As we discovered, we were in a position that was pretty much left alone, aside from some pretty ineffective shelling, from which we were able to shield ourselves, and bursts of artillery fire that caused limited damage and which we were able to return with interest. They certainly weren't full-blooded attacks that we experienced in those early days on the line, but our time would come.

We still had to send out patrols, though, including standing patrols to a small trench just 300 or 400 yards in front of our position. The main purpose was to act as an early warning, tucked away in a small trench and ready to raise the alarm if there was imminent danger. You had to be alert and ready to think on your feet when you landed on a standing patrol. A false alarm could cause as much of a furore as a full-scale alert, so you had to be sure before the shout went out. You would sit there all night in your wee dugout, listening and hoping you would get through without incident. All of the positions were protected by barbed wire, stretching out along our territory, but it would serve only to delay a determined enemy force rather than hold them back.

On my first night out in the paddy in front of our position, I heard the 'clink-clank' that became such a familiar noise in the months ahead. It was the sound of weaponry somewhere out in front of you, in the darkness. The key was determining how far ahead it was and which direction it was heading in. That night, I have to admit, the noise sent a shiver down my spine. It was so still, so calm, and the metallic chiming made it feel as though the enemy was yards away from our trench. All of a sudden, it didn't feel so safe.

I was all for reaching for my own weapon, but fortunately I had an experienced lance corporal with me. He assured me that it would be a North Korean patrol passing along the line rather than trying to breach it, that the noise would keep on moving away. He was right. In truth, I don't think I would have had the confidence to open fire on my first night out even if we had caught sight of them.

You can have all the training you like, go through all the practice – nothing really prepares you for the feeling you have when you are sent out armed and on active service for the first time. It carries a lot of responsibility and sets your mind racing. You know at some point you will have to fire in anger, but the big question racing through your mind is 'When?'

We came back to our position and reported what we believed to have been the sound of an enemy patrol, doing exactly as we had been doing on the opposite side of the line, but explained we had not had clear sight and had not engaged. Details were carefully logged of every contact with the enemy.

Not that it was only the Chinese and North Koreans we had to worry about. We had the Americans to keep us on our toes too.

There had been cases where British patrols had been fired at by the Yanks, and the Canadian troops had been shot up too. The Americans weren't the most subtle soldiers out there and certainly didn't do much to hide their presence. Generally, you could hear them before you saw them – although I declined to shoot that lot too.

It's fair to say there was an element of mistrust out in the field, and sure enough we were caught in the firing line out on patrol. I kicked up hell when the dust settled. We were on the same side, after all, and it was crazy to be so reckless. I can't imagine just opening up on a group without being certain who was in the line of fire. You're not going to win a war by taking one decision that is wrong or right. It is a long-drawn-out affair and restraint is crucial. Better to be sitting here writing and talking about it than trying to play the hero and getting caught in a firefight.

Fortunately, we settled in a higher position, still within 100 yards of our original spot but with the added safety of elevated ground. Generally speaking, we were not on fighting patrols at that stage, but it didn't mean you wouldn't get caught up in sporadic outbreaks even in those protected positions. On these warning patrols, it was fine to be told, 'Quiet now, nobody put your tip above the gun position and let's see what develops,' but if they'd had a bad experience prior to that, then understandably people got twitchy.

Eventually, after a couple of days to find our feet, we changed positions and were trucked down to the bottom of a nearby hill. As usual with these switches, it was all done under cover of darkness. You did your best to keep a grasp of where you were, but it wasn't easy.

We were ordered to climb to a position at the top of a path. It was a long and winding trail, right to the top of the hill, and we discovered we were relieving an American squad who had been on duty there. Only they didn't want to wait – our feet had barely touched the ground, clambering off the back of the trucks, when there was a huge outbreak of fire – everything from small arms to the Browning heavy machine guns they loved so much. As we began to pick up the pace to get in position, hand grenades started raining over our heads and landing in the gully beyond the path we were following. You could hear the giggles coming from the Yanks. It was their little bit of fun to celebrate the end of their stint in the line – fine if you're carefree and on your way for a bit of R&R back at base, not so good when you're heading in the opposite direction and you've now got half the Chinese army setting their sights on your position.

By the time we got to the top of the hill, there were shells coming back across the paddy from the Chinese, bombarding the position on the back of the final flourish from the US troops. There had been no tactical thought behind their grand fireworks display; it was simply a case of getting rid of all their ammunition so they didn't have to carry it back off the hill. Of course, those on the receiving end had no idea, and were busy retaliating with everything they could find to fire in our direction.

It was a more exposed position than we had been used to, and the gunfire was getting through and ricocheting all around us. You have to have your wits about you, protect yourself as best you can and get through the night. We did that, even if we were shaken up by it all, and saw it through to the quieter daylight hours when nobody wanted to break cover for fear of being spotted.

The sense of anticipation never really abated. It was the same the last time going out on the line as it had been stepping out for the first time. Being a corporal, I had to take a patrol out after a couple of days, to get my bearings and settle into the role. Fortunately, a few of my comrades had been in the position for a decent length of time and I was able to fall back on their knowledge of the terrain and the layout of the area. Everyone would chip in and help you out.

WELCOME TO THE FRONT LINE

It was incredible how quickly we all settled into the life on the line. It became routine to be shot at and equally normal to have a gun in your hand and use it in anger. This was war now, and we were in it for the long haul.

5

THE HORRORS OF WAR

IT IS IMPOSSIBLE TO SERVE on the front line in a battle zone and not encounter the horrors of war. I saw a man shot dead yards just from where I was standing, I watched napalm do its horrible work and I suffered the pain of being gunned down myself. However, I would not class any of those as the most disturbing events of my time in Korea.

No, for me the most harrowing episode revolved around a man I never knew. He was someone I saw only once, fleetingly, but I will never forget his face for as long as I draw breath.

It was during a stint out on the Hook that I encountered the situation that still haunts me to this day. On patrol, I came across one of our lads running along the top of the trenches, heading in a direction that would have taken him away from the line.

I stopped him in his tracks and asked him what on earth he thought he was doing, up there in the line of fire like a sitting duck. He told me, 'I've had enough,' and pushed me aside, carrying on the way he had been running before I'd intercepted him.

The next day, I heard the news I had been half expecting: my man was dead; a shell had landed right in his path and killed him instantly.

The way he was going, it was pretty much inevitable. We were being watched all of the time. Under cover of the trenches, our pits or even the hooches, we were relatively well protected. Out on top, so highly visible, there was no such insurance. The enemy must have thought it was Christmas come early to be presented with a target that, although moving, was laid bare for them. Whether by shell or by bullet, they would have hunted him down soon enough, without a flicker of hesitation.

Perhaps he knew that himself; surely he must have done. He obviously thought it was a gamble worth taking, as, one way or another, he'd be out of a situation that he obviously loathed. Thinking rationally is not always possible when you're embedded in such difficult circumstances, with no time to analyse things, and it is hard to imagine exactly what must have been going on in his head as he made his run for it.

Could I have done more to stop him? Most certainly. I could have punched him in the jaw and dragged him back to safety – anything to stop what looked certain to be a grisly end. But I didn't. He was determined to carry on and I let him. I don't even know his name, but I still feel a sense of responsibility for what happened.

More than half a century on, I still play the scenario out in my mind. I could have saved him; I could have made the difference. In a split second, I made a decision that changed the course of that man's life. He was cut down in his prime, like so many others out in Korea.

I suppose what was running through my head at the time was: what I would have wanted if the boot had been on the other foot? If it was me who made the decision to cut my losses and run, would I have taken kindly to somebody standing in my way? Not a chance. I'd have pushed on through and nobody would have stopped me.

We were all adults; everyone has a right to make their own choices and in essence shape their own destiny. He took his chances and made a break for it – if he had succeeded, got himself away from the line and somehow managed to get a ticket home, then he would have got his wish and been spared another day on the line. Unfortunately for him, war doesn't always give you the ending you'd hoped for. It was a little too late to decide to become a conscientious objector.

He had the look of a troubled soul as he barged past me on the line, and I shudder to think what he went through as he picked his way past the pits and made his bid to free himself from his torment. He never stood a chance, the poor soul. The only tiny consolation, if there can be such a thing, is that he would have known very little about it. When a shell strikes, there's no pause for thought.

It's impossible to guess exactly what his train of thought was that night, but I would be willing to bet that it wasn't a spur-of-the-moment decision or some sort of sudden breakdown. Even before we'd set a boot on Korean soil, it was possible to pick out those who were going to find it difficult to cope with the demands about to be placed upon them. Maybe not enough was done to get them the help they needed before it had gone too far. If there had been some sort of mechanism in place, then there's no doubt tragedy could have been averted on more than one occasion.

I was fortunate that I wanted to be there in the thick of it. Not everyone shared that mindset. There was one guy, from Crieff, who we could all see was struggling from the first day we enlisted at Perth. When we went up to the Highlands to learn weaponry and all the rest at Fort George, he was told in no uncertain terms, 'Look, son, unless you get a grip of yourself, there's going to be big trouble – not just for you but for the rest of the company.'

It's one thing to tell someone to pull themselves together and smarten up their act, quite another to make it happen. Sure enough, out in Korea, he was blown up when he was cleaning grenades. He killed himself and one other, with another badly wounded.

That is the danger of having people who just aren't cut out for it. Although that's an extreme example, there were other incidents and accidents along the way that provided an argument against forcing people into it.

You quickly learn that your life isn't in your own hands; a big share of the responsibility is with those around you. The last thing you want is to look to your side and see someone who's a nervous wreck. The thing is, you end up being saddled with them regardless of whether they want to be there or not.

That's where the argument about sending criminals into the army as part of their rehabilitation falls down – it's all very well saying, 'We're going to make soldiers out of you,' but there has to be a physical and mental toughness there to begin with. The last thing you want is to be posted alongside a bunch of idle or disruptive convicts, although perhaps placing one or two in a regiment might be effective and help them to tread a new path. Managed the right way, I do still think there's a place for national service for all – not this idea that it should be reserved for those who have done something wrong. That sends out completely the wrong message, in my opinion.

It was telling that our friend from Crieff was singled out during our stint in the Highlands as a potential problem; it's just a shame the training we went through up there didn't set him straight. Some of the conscripts who didn't necessarily fancy army life did grow into it, though, and by the time we reached Korea were fully fledged, fully committed soldiers. Some remained unconvinced but made the best of what they considered to be a bad lot and just got on with the job in hand. A tiny minority simply could never embrace any aspect of army life.

When you consider some of the things that went on, it was a hard sell at times. I can remember being given a jolt when a low-flying aircraft thundered overhead while we were out on the line. The noise hit us before we caught sight of it and for a split second there was panic while we waited to see whose plane it was. It was one of ours, fortunately, and we could relax.

Then it dawned on us what its sortie was all about, with the distinctive oval napalm canisters fluttering beneath the plane as it flew over the enemy lines. The way they wobbled through the air was unmistakable. The feeling you got when you watched them hit the hills across the way was far from euphoric. Napalm is horrible, horrible stuff, and I knew all too well the devastating effect it would have on any unfortunate soul who came into contact with it.

We had been shelled by napalm ourselves, or at least the enemy equivalent, and I pitied any of the poor buggers who found themselves underneath our little delivery of those deadly parcels. We knew from experience that it didn't matter where you were, in trenches or even in a hooch, the stuff could find a way to you. It would burn clothes, flesh and anything else in its path, and there was no way to put it out. It has to be one of the most evil inventions of our time. The thought of that or any other chemical warfare makes my stomach turn. It changed the rules of engagement forever.

Napalm was still relatively new when we were in its shadow in Korea. It had been around since midway through the Second World War, and it had not taken long for its horrific properties to become apparent. It was an American creation and manufactured in huge quantities for their use in Korea; more than a quarter of a million pounds of the stuff was directed at tanks and enemy positions every day. It would torch anything in its path and was almost impossible to extinguish – a harrowing thing to be on the receiving end of.

The Americans would later make great claims about its effectiveness, citing the fact that droves of Chinese and North Korean men would surrender on the back of each of their napalm raids, throwing up the white flags and being captured when the next wave of planes appeared overhead, but even so I would question its use.

As far as the US chiefs were concerned, it was just another weapon in their armoury and was there to be used for any gain they could make. So they used it, and far from sparingly. The Second World War had been a testing ground; this was the full roll-out for them and their air crews.

It may sound strange for a man who was out there among guns, bullets and shells to be questioning what, in essence, was just another tool for the allied forces to use. The difference in my mind was that with traditional artillery you had a fighting chance of defending yourself, whether with speed of thought or tactical decisions, whereas with napalm there was little you could do. If it was coming in your direction, you were consigned to disastrous consequences, and even in the grim circumstances of war that was brutal. It really is something you wouldn't wish on your worst enemy, quite literally.

All we could do was watch and listen as the napalm fluttered down across the paddy and wonder just how heavy a toll it would take when it reached its target. It was uncomfortable for all of us, but it was just another part of day-to-day life in Korea during the conflict.

A so-called 'safer' derivative was developed by the Americans after the Korean War but if you remember the protests surrounding the use of napalm during the Vietnam War you get an idea that the opposition never went away . . . not surprisingly. Even now, I've read reports that it has been used in Iraq and Afghanistan by US forces – something they have been at great pains to deny. Whatever the truth, I know from my own experience how fearsome a weapon it is.

There were many Scottish soldiers who found out to far greater cost what the consequences of its use were. A crew from the Argyll and Sutherland Highlanders was hit accidentally by a napalm attack during an operation in 1950. It was known as the Battle of Hill 282. They'd asked for air support, not realising what would result when the US fighters were scrambled with their 'special' weapon.

Mind you, the air force men suffered themselves, of course, and there were quite a few losses of lives and planes during the conflict. As recently as 2011 there were reports of remains of an RAF pilot being discovered in North Korea and repatriated after the authorities did the honourable thing, allowing him to be identified and afforded the dignity of a proper funeral.

I've read about remains of US soldiers being discovered in South Korea, too, by villagers minding their own business and just going for a stroll along the beach. It was a nasty, nasty business and the reminders are all around. It is incredible to think that, more than half a century later, the terrible after-effects of the Korean War are still being felt in so many ways, by so many people and in countries on different continents as the pieces continue to be picked up and the ramifications are felt.

What we shouldn't lose sight of is the root cause. Although the Chinese were increasingly involved, there was little doubt it was the North Koreans who were the main aggressors – they were a vicious fighting force intent on maximum damage. There was no mercy, and fire had to be met with fire.

Of course, the other thing that shouldn't be forgotten is that it was not just servicemen who experienced the full horror of the war. The civilian population of South Korea was subjected to some barbaric treatment. That was one of the key reasons we were involved in the first place. There would, I am sure, have been civilian casualties in the North, too, although that was something we did everything in our power to avoid. The events of the war continue to reverberate, with the Americans staging an inquiry in the late 1990s into mass killings north of Seoul early in the war.

We were sent in to peg back the aggressive North Korean

attack and restore stability. Everyone who served out there, including me, can feel pride and satisfaction that our efforts were not in vain. For well over 50 years, the peace we battled to establish held firm, albeit in tense circumstances. It wasn't until the North launched its attacks on the South in 2010 that the bad old days threatened to return.

When North Korea shelled Yeonpyeong Island and killed four people, including two civilians, the media coverage went into overdrive and the memories came flooding back for me. The island they targeted was near to their own waters, in an area that has been disputed since the war ended in the 1950s. Clearly, the settlement terms still rankle with the regime in the North. The fact that their actions led to villagers over the border being evacuated to safer locations tells its own story: there's obviously still a nagging fear that the situation could escalate on any given day.

The difference in 2010 was that South Korea was able to scramble its own fighter jets and make use of its own bunkers in defence, able to deter the aggression from the North on its own this time – although the claim at the time was that it was military exercises carried out by the South that had provoked their neighbours in the first place. It wouldn't take much to reignite the old border tensions, which obviously still remain. The sound of artillery fire in the near distance would be just about enough to spark off another skirmish.

Of course, the threat of a nuclear response by the North put an entirely different complexion on the recent troubles. Once again, the Americans and British waded in, diplomatically this time rather than with manpower, and once again it was China that was allied with the North. The more things change, the more they stay the same.

It is impossible to predict whether the uneasy peace that has existed in Korea since my time there will remain intact. There's a new leader in place in the North, and second-guessing the direction he will take his country in is impossible. In the years ahead, there will undoubtedly be changes and developments in the relationship with the South. What I do know is that I hope they never see a return to the all-out war that we experienced.

6

THE HOOK

RONSON AND WARSAW. A FIRM of solicitors perhaps? Maybe a dentist's practice, or could it be a publisher of fine books? In fact, those are two names to strike fear and loathing into the heart of any British soldier who served during the Korean War. They were the names given to two key positions on that most vital of battlegrounds, the Hook.

The Hook in itself has become synonymous with the war. It has gone down in history, inspiring artwork and books. The name sounds intriguing, maybe even romantic, but, believe me, the reality was very different. The Hook was a long, half-moon-shaped ridge, a sprawling area that both sides viewed as tactically vital, right on the line. If you held it, you had a huge advantage; it was particularly vital for our forces in holding firm and preventing the Chinese and North Koreans from advancing south.

As a result, it was the scene of the fiercest fighting for the duration of the war and is said to have been won and lost at least 20 times. Thousands of men were lost in the process, the victims of the Hook.

In among the hills and valleys of the Korean countryside, surroundings that we Scots felt very much at home in, not least because of the cold and damp of the harsh winter, the Hook, near the Samichon River, dominated the area. Tanks were useless because of the hilly territory, so it was all down to artillery and infantry attacks to hold it.

In the bleakest of seasons, the vegetation was drab and dank, with a layer of dust and debris from the constant shelling adding to the desolation all around us. It was a grim setting for some grim events, but somehow the surroundings became almost comforting as you got to know every inch of the ground and its many quirks. The potholes, the contours, the undergrowth ... they all served as markers, familiar points of reference that could prove very useful in the dead of night when you were scrambling for cover.

In theory, the Chinese and Koreans could have held an advantage, given that it was more familiar territory to them than it was to us, and because they knew the climate and conditions. But it didn't always work that way, and before too long you made it your own, learning how to use the features and finding paths and routes that became second nature when you were out on the line.

The Hook had been the scene of plenty of bloody skirmishes throughout the war, but it is those known as the First, Second and Third Battles of the Hook that have gone down as the decisive moments. These took place during the period from the autumn of 1952 to May the following year.

My own experience of the fabled Hook came between the second and third battles, when C Company was moved up at very short notice. The A Company had suffered a hell of a night out there and had been overrun, taking a lot of casualties in the process. They won the day eventually, but it had taken its toll and they were pulled back from the line to regroup and tend to the wounded.

We hadn't really come into close contact with the enemy up to that point, other than the shells that had been peppered in our direction and them rattling off equipment in the paddy. Given that the majority of C Company were conscripts like me, none among our number had any solid close-combat experience, so it was always going to be a steep learning curve for us all.

My memories of that time are of how crystal clear the nights were, with the stars shining in the sky and an eerie silence descending over the line. It was cold, it was still and it was so, so very quiet. In the distance, there was still the clinking of weapons, which sent a shiver down your spine no matter how often you heard it. They were out there; we just didn't know where or how close.

The daytime was far less stressful. You could rely on line of sight to gauge danger. It would take a brave, or foolish, commander to send his men forward without the cover of darkness, so we could relax, to an extent, when the sun was up. But as it set, and the night fell, tension would rise and your senses were heightened. The slightest movement glimpsed out of the corner of your eye, a noise in the distance – everything was a potential danger and treated as such.

We occupied a position on the right flank of the Hook, where we were subjected to regular shelling. It was fairly indiscriminate stuff, with the bombardment aimed in our general direction and taking out anything in its path. If they got close, they'd take down sections of our defences, sending the dust flying – and soldiers scampering for cover. Other shells were less troublesome, sailing away into the wilderness.

The advantage we had was that the hooches were well built and you felt safe enough in those. They were built into the reverse side of the hill, so the shells firing towards us tended to sail over the roof and into the valley behind. The worry came when they used mortars, which instead of following the gradual arc of the shells tended to fire straight up and steeply down on top of your position. With those, there was far less protection.

You grew to learn from the sound whether it was a shell or a mortar heading in your direction and could shelter accordingly. You never switched off. The violent explosion of the shells and the softer sound of the mortars – almost a 'pffft' sort of noise – live with me to this day. I can replay those sounds in my mind as if it were yesterday, and I well remember that feeling of nervousness between hearing it and discovering where it was going to crash to earth and wreak havoc. You listened, you watched and you waited.

From our position tucked away on the Hook, we were asked to supply a patrol for Ronson. One word, just a collection of letters, but a word that struck genuine terror into the heart of many a soldier during the war.

As I mentioned, Ronson and Warsaw were the two key outposts on the Hook. Both were loathed by the troops, who knew they were stepping into real peril when asked to man either of them. Warsaw was, to my mind, the less dangerous of the pair. It was tucked away into our lines, a long and gently sloping position that at least offered a degree of cover. Ronson, on the other hand, stuck out like a sore thumb in front of our central position. I hadn't experienced it, but I had heard about it. In reality, I didn't know what I was letting myself in for.

Ronson was the most vital part of our defence, and the patrols were shared by all of the companies, regardless of their place on the line. I was asked to do the Ronson patrol once, twice, three times. Warsaw I covered only twice.

Ronson was a standing patrol and we were in contact with HQ by radio. The procedure if attacked or bypassed by the enemy was to wire HQ, shout 'Hell's a-poppin!' and then you had just 30 seconds to get back to your own line and escape the artillery barrage that would follow.

Now, that doesn't sound like a long time at all. You can trust me when I say that it seems an awful lot less when you're down there on the ground in pitch darkness, running for your life, laden down with weapons and kit while all the time trying to avoid the boulders, branches and potholes littering the path back to safety. Run was what you were told to do, and run we did when that familiar cry went up.

Whenever I meet somebody from the battalion and ask if they were ever at Ronson, that's the first thing they will say: 'Hell's a-poppin'.' I had the dubious privilege of making that call on one occasion, during the second trip I made to Ronson.

While we were stuck out there, the familiar clink-clank drew closer – a Chinese patrol was upon us before we knew it. First we could hear them, soon we could see them marching towards us. Staying still and trying to sit out the approach was a non-starter; the enemy would have found our position easily enough and would have been in about us quick smart. They thought nothing of storming gun pits or trenches and there had been a number of instances of hand-to-hand combat ensuing in positions once the attackers had been disarmed.

We weren't going to hang about and let that happen, so, as instructed in this situation, the call went up: 'Hell's a-poppin'!' We turned on our heels and the shells started landing where we had been standing just seconds earlier, with us heading for safety and the Chinese, not quite knowing what had hit them, scattering back in the direction they had come as they desperately tried to get out of the line of fire.

To be fair, I knew exactly how they felt. The Chinese gave as good as they got, as bitter experience proved. Which brings me to my third trip to Ronson.

We weren't on the front line all the time we were out there. We were shuffled back and forth to make sure we got decent rest and recuperation time in between the pretty intense periods of fighting. One of the extended rests I got was a ten-day stint away from the line to take part in a football tournament (more on that later), and it was when I was recovering from that that I got the call to go out again.

The A Company, who themselves had not been long back at the front, found themselves being fiercely attacked on the Hook, so C Company were called up for emergency cover. The cry had gone out for help and we had to respond *tout de suite*. We were crowded into Bren gun carriers and headed at full speed for the Hook, just a couple of miles from our starting point. It might have been a short distance, but it felt as if it took a lifetime.

To put you in the picture, the Bren gun carrier made for one of the most terrifying modes of transport imaginable when you were in a war zone. Those little armoured vehicles, basically track-driven open-top tanks, could cover the ground fine, but as we battered through heavy shelling and massive mortar fire, it was what was falling from the sky rather than the earth beneath us that was our major concern. With no roof, you were effectively travelling in a big metal box – just perfect for collecting incoming fire. It was like a high-stakes game of hoopla.

We were bouncing along knowing that if one of those things landed at our feet we would be wiped out. It would be like lobbing a firework in a biscuit tin and standing back to watch what happened. All the time, I was willing the driver to get his bloody foot down and get us out of there.

There's no doubt we were saved by the ground around us during that episode, with shells splattering into the soft mud, the blasts absorbed by it. If the terrain had been firmer, it would have been a very different story. We drove down that track with our hearts in our mouths, the journey just about as treacherous as the line we were heading for.

We reached the Hook and piled out of the back of the Bren carrier. The sky was lit up with shells and all sorts. It was like Bonfire Night. The instruction went out to climb the back of the Hook, go through the trenches and retake Ronson. Now we knew what we were there for. Would it be third time lucky for me and old Ronson? It wasn't quite like coming home, that's for sure.

We reached the jumping-off spot then made our move out of the trenches towards Ronson. There was a barrage of field-gun fire, an extreme attack coming in low. The Germans had their 88-mm in the Second World War and, as we found out, the Koreans had their equivalent. They could take out tanks and sure as hell could do major damage to our positions and anyone who got in the way.

We were working out of trenches, which were waist high at the very most, with a slight rise behind and a wire screening for extra protection. The field guns were battering that wire, coming up through the gully and going at it hard. Ronson was way out there and they were in the hollow trying to get through the wires, with heavy fire from us as we tried to peg them back and hold our place.

I pulled the trigger to attack the enemy often enough during my time on the line, but that night was different. That was the biggest battle I was involved in out there and my gun was red hot.

It isn't an aspect of the war I am particularly comfortable talking about, and certainly not one I would ever brag about. I was never one for trying to find out whom I had hit or what damage had been done; I preferred not to know, in all honesty. We were all at war, so I make no apologies for firing in anger, but I wouldn't say I took satisfaction from it. It wasn't a game; there were no points to be scored. It was all about making sure that when we went out on the line we came back with the same number of men as we'd gone out with. In the main, we did exactly that, and I would do whatever it took to make sure that happened. In a choice between them or us, there was only ever one answer.

The night we went out to reclaim Ronson was one of fearsome fighting, some at very close quarters. The position had been overrun by the Chinese and we had to go in heavy to force them back, a real blitz. They in turn were retaliating with everything they had, including grenades.

The Chinese and Korean forces came armed with what were known as 'tattie mashers' – stick-mounted grenades similar to those that had been favoured by the Germans in the Second World War – and I got very close to one of those when it came sailing into the trench we were firing from. Because the dugout was shallow, probably two or three feet at most, we were lying prone when this thing bounced in among us. It was live and it was right there in front of us, just out of my reach. The lad next to me in the trench was called Davie Robertson, and he saved my life that night. Davie, quick as a flash, managed to reach down to where the grenade was nestled, just next to his boot, and grab hold of it, lobbing it back in the direction from which it had come. Before it had even touched the ground on the other side of the trench, it exploded, full force, in mid-air. If Davie had been just seconds later in grabbing the grenade, it would have been the end of us. You usually had until the count of seven from the time one was activated to the time it detonated, so there was no hanging about or thinking about it. Pure instinct was what you had to rely on.

I have to say I threw a few of my own grenades that night; it was the only time I had to while I was out on the line. The enemy troops were very close to the position we were fighting our way out of and there was no option but to try to clear them out any way we could. I threw a few grenades over the left-hand side of our position and all I know is we ended up alive, which was the main objective.

To a man, everyone fought tooth and nail to peg them back, and we came through to retake Ronson and, more crucially, the Hook in general. When the morning broke, there were Chinese and North Korean soldiers lying on the wire dead, hanging there where they had been hit as they tried to clamber over to get at us.

There were heavy, heavy casualties on the enemy side and sadly some on ours too.

Some had made it across the gully where there were occasional gaps in our defence, and, as the light began to filter through from the rising sun, we could see there were two Chinese soldiers in the trench beside us. One was dead, one wasn't.

The one who had survived the night's fighting, if only just, was groaning and moaning in agony. He didn't look to be in any condition to trouble us, but when the atmosphere is as charged as it is in those circumstances you still worry. What if he was a suicide case, just ready to reach for his belt and pull the pin?

Before I had time to think, a single shot rang out from no more than a couple of men behind me in the line that was filtering along the trench. I didn't know who had opened fire, didn't want to know. He did what every one of us had considered and pulled the trigger as he walked past. I wasn't seriously tempted to do the same, but you can't blame a guy for taking the action he did.

Understandably, tensions were running high, and they were intensifying. Then the officer in charge of us said to pass the word back that we were turning to our right over the trench and up towards our target. That was when we went over the top and eventually got out to Ronson, recapturing it in a blaze of fire and a flurry of grenades.

It was typical of the type of skirmish that happened week in and week out during the war. And then there were those periods when the full battles took place. The First Battle of the Hook took place in October 1952, with heavy casualties on both sides. It was the first in a gruelling series of conflicts fought at regular intervals. Even when these died down, the positions in that area were constantly engaged with Chinese and North Korean forces in the near distance. They would crank out shells from their positions on the hillside opposite before scurrying back into their defensive dugouts with their weapons, making it difficult to get at either the equipment or the men.

It was to become a problem for the Black Watch to tackle, as the regiment was called forward in November 1952 to take its turn defending the Hook. Lieutenant Colonel David Rose was charged with leading the operation.

We relieved the US Marines and there was a lot of work to be done in rebuilding trenches and laying the wire that would serve as protection. What had once been deeply dug, heavily fortified havens had been reduced to rubble, which by all accounts was ankle deep in places. It took a hell of a lot of elbow grease and sheer spirit by Black Watch troops to restore the safety measures and return that section of the line to a workable location, with physical defences to match those provided by the massed ranks of our soldiers. The rebuilding of the trenches and gun pits was to prove hugely important to all of the men who went on to serve at the Hook in the latter stages of the war, and I know my company and I benefited from it when we arrived to join the cause.

It was back-breaking donkey work to create the infrastructure – a hidden and unglamorous aspect of every war that often goes unremarked. The Black Watch undertook those tasks with aplomb before being forced into more pressing action.

Soon after arriving, the regiment became embroiled in the Second Battle of the Hook, which began on 18 November 1952. Tens of thousands of rounds were volleyed back and forth, with the Chinese threatening to overrun our boys on more than one occasion. The fighting raged through the night, but eventually the spirit of the Black Watch prevailed and they regained the foothold that was so necessary.

There were times when it looked as though the enemy would burst through and push the allied forces back, sending them running for cover. Thankfully, they were pegged back during that particular assault, struggling to breach a well-drilled and determined group of men. The Black Watch had been given a specific task – to retain the Hook – and the consensus was that nobody would give up, no matter how heavy the barrage was or how close at hand our opposite number was.

By all accounts, our boys could hear the sound of Chinese bugles signalling the start of another wave of attacks. When the enemy was thwarted by the wire defences, they resorted, among other tactics, to lobbing grenades in among our troops. It was in the early hours of the morning of 19 November that the battle was eventually won. The staying power of the Black Watch soldiers was credited in all reports as the reason for the positive outcome. There were plenty of casualties, some wounded and some killed, but losses on the Chinese side were far greater.

The Third Battle of the Hook came on the night of 28–29 May 1953, just a short time after I had been taken down while defending our corner. Had I not been hospitalised, I would have been there among the Black Watch troops for the battle.

Hours and hours of shelling preceded a charge by the Chinese, leading to close-quarter fighting in which the enemy was to discover that the Black Watch was a force to be reckoned with. Once again, they were repelled.

It was said that the enemy hit our positions with 11,000 shells during the course of a single hour on 28 May. That tells you something about the level of determination with which they were fighting the war. Comparisons were made with the First World War, such was the brutal and relentless style employed by the Chinese and North Koreans. They did not succeed, however, losing an estimated 2,000 men in that third battle alone.

The less well-known Fourth Battle of the Hook took place right on the cusp of the ceasefire in 1953. The death toll was even greater in that conflict, with 3,000 Chinese troops dead once the dust had cleared. It was said to have taken five days for the enemy's stretcher parties to clear the area of bodies. Horrible, horrible stuff.

When I look at photographs of the Hook now I can still picture myself there with the rest of the boys, living on our wits and doing what we could to stay clear of trouble. I have a handful of old photos that I dig out from time to time and have a peek at. They were taken on cameras borrowed and shared on the line and further back, moments in time captured for posterity, and I'm glad they were. You never realise what you're living through at the time, but as the years roll past the significance dawns on you.

I often wonder what became of the positions we left behind when peace finally took hold, to the trenches and the pits that were so painstakingly carved into that piece of hillside. Could you still pick out Ronson, or has it been lost to the sands of time? Are the walls of Warsaw still standing, or were they flattened before our troops returned home?

I've never been back to Korea since I left on a stretcher many moons ago – never been close. Part of me thinks it would be interesting to retrace my steps from the war years, tramp back up the Hook and admire the view without fear of being picked off by enemy fire, but another part of me thinks it is better to let sleeping dogs lie.

Nowadays, you can buy paintings and prints depicting the area; a little market has sprung up in Korean War memories. For those of us who served there, the clearest pictures are those locked away in our memory banks. Once experienced, never forgotten.

7

IT'S A RAT'S LIFE

WHEN YOU ARE EMBEDDED IN battle, half-frozen and deprived of sleep, there are few moments to look forward to in the day. Mealtimes were among them, surprisingly enough.

Granted, it wasn't quite fine dining, but when you're cold and hungry that doesn't matter a jot. Back at the camps, there were proper cooking tents on the go, with decent grub, but while we were out on the line we relied on ration packs, and particularly the self-heating cans that had been fixtures with the Allied Forces during the Second World War. The tins had a ring pull on them and when you tugged it open it triggered a warming mechanism, some sort of chemical reaction in a chamber surrounding the food that gave off heat to cook up the contents. It wasn't new technology; climbers, explorers and the like had used it before the Army.

What I quickly came to appreciate was that cooking the contents of the can gave you a rare burst of warmth. You could cup your hands round it for a brief respite from the icy conditions. No doubt the mountaineers savoured the same sensation when they sat down to eat. The food wasn't all that bad, either – be it beans or a stew or some other sort of meat – and it was one of the few bright spots in the day when you could break for those rations and build your strength back up.

The Americans had huge supplies with them and would pass things on to the various forces, adapted to suit each nationality. The French got more bread, the Asian troops got more rice and spices, while we Brits made do with grub very similar to the Yanks'. It was all about keeping people mentally and physically strong, and there's no better way to do that for a soldier than through his belly.

The tins, it turned out, had a triple use out on the line. Obviously, they fed us, and they functioned, if briefly, as heaters. The third, most ingenious use was as a makeshift early-warning system, long before electronic motion sensors had been devised. What would happen was that guys would wolf down their food and once the warmth had gone out of the metal and the tins were no use any more they'd throw them in front of the gun pits – maybe 30 or 40 yards ahead of them, down against the wire. That way, if any of the Chinese or Korean troops did manage to breach the defences and get through the wire they'd stumble over a pile of cans and set off a clatter of noise to give us a heads up and let us get our rifles trained on them.

One thing we hadn't bargained on was a different type of enemy: the dreaded Korean rats. They'd go foraging for scraps among the old food tins and send them jingling – the problem being that we didn't know whether it was rats or soldiers coming for us. We'd be reaching for the guns in the blink of an eye, and there were some merry panics at all hours of the day and night because of that little system. Not such a bright idea after all.

Now, the bloody rats in that part of the world are as big as cats, and they caused no end of problems for us, far worse than shredding our nerves with their noisy searches for food. To start with, these things used to come out at night and when we were sleeping in the hooches it was a nightmare. The way our little 'houses' were built, there were roof beams set across the top and then layers of sandbags on top to absorb any blasts and give a bit of insulation from the worst of the frost. Where the sandbags met the ground, which was a dusty sort of earth, there was a small lip as the roofs sloped into the hillside. The rats would bury themselves in that ridge of earth – just at the level that the top bunk was generally at on the inside. You would be lying in bed and you'd hear scratching, then feel a shower of dust falling on you.

Bearing in mind it was pitch black, all you were going on was what you could hear. So you'd light a candle – and find one of those great big beasts staring back at you. It would get a fright and go back into its hole, then pop back out and stare at you. You quickly realised that they weren't in the least bit frightened of us hardy soldiers.

I'm not a squeamish type; I'm a fisherman, after all. Dealing with catches has never been a problem, and I've grown up in the great outdoors, so wildlife doesn't bother me. But these rats were a different story; they were enough to make your stomach turn. Even the thought of them made your flesh creep, especially when it was dark and you didn't know whether they were crawling around you or not.

In the hooches, you'd reach for your bayonet at first sight of one of those monster rats. You'd throw a blade like some sort of circus act, but the rat would always pop its head back into its hidey-hole just in time. It went on night after night, to the point where you wouldn't get a proper sleep because you were waiting for that telltale scraping sound and for the roof to start falling on you.

People tried all sorts of things to get the blighters, but very few succeeded. I've even read about some of the troops using grenades to try to blast them in their burrows out in the field. Whether it was bayonets, bullets or anything else we threw at them, they kept on coming back for more. And coming back again and again . . .

As much as they were loathsome creatures and real nuisances, it was far more serious than just an irritation. They weren't scared of us, at least not half as scared as we had to be of them. Manchurian fever was becoming a massive worry for our forces out in Korea, and the rats were the prime carriers. If you were bitten by one of those blighters, you had a first-class ticket home, no questions asked. The medics were taking it seriously and quite rightly so – a lot of men lost their lives.

It wasn't just if you were bitten that you had to be worried. It was thought that the fever could also be carried through food contaminated by the rats or even by the mites carried by them. Our four-legged friends would crawl over the food, the mites would be left behind, an unsuspecting soldier would take a bite – you can fill in the rest yourself. There has also been research suggesting the fever was airborne, emanating from the urine and faeces of the rats and other carriers (breeds of mice and voles were also identified as sources) that were present on the ground and undergrowth.

Korean hemorrhagic fever was another name the condition went by. At first, a sufferer experienced only flu-like symptoms and drowsiness. What followed was far more severe. Next came sickness, then dizziness, swollen eyelids and a burning throat, followed by stomach cramps and then the onset of the collapse of the internal organs and all that went with that.

They tried their best to treat it in the field, but all too often it was impossible. There was an element of mystery about the illness; nobody knew exactly what it was or was 100 per cent sure how to treat it. In fact, at one stage it was feared the plague had returned and would sweep through the population, including us troops, in Korea.

It was the Japanese army who had first diagnosed it, while serving in Manchuria in 1939. Even now, there's no cure, and in the 1980s the Americans were hit by a virtually identical strain of it when some of their Marines, out in Korea on exercise, were struck down. Two of them died and many others became ill, showing just how stubborn the dreaded fever was, sticking around all that time. Flamethrowers had even been used after the war to torch the brush and ground in the hope of killing it off, but this clearly wasn't successful.

In the 1950s, there were hundreds of cases across the various nationalities out there, and I believe roughly one in every ten of those died. They set up special field hospitals specifically to deal with the fever cases, which were far more prevalent than malaria or the other nasties that were doing the rounds. Manchurian fever deaths were horrible ones, with haemorrhaging of the internal organs the ultimate fate of the unlucky ones.

It has been suggested that the high death rates in the prisoner of war camps run by the Chinese and North Koreans could have been down to the fever. It makes sense. If the disease was festering in the open countryside, the far more squalid camps would certainly be prone to it. There were terrible tales from the camps, as you would expect.

In contrast, in our own camps the health of our forces was relatively good, with few outbreaks or serious illnesses to deal with. When you consider so many men were living in close quarters, in foreign climes and in such extreme weather conditions, it is amazing there weren't more frequent problems.

Apparently, the Americans sent members of their medical corps out to catch rabbits, mice, rats and anything else suspected of carrying Manchurian fever so they could carry out tests and try to get to the bottom of it. The rats, not surprisingly, were the prime suspects, with ticks also reported to be carriers.

However it was transmitted, you didn't want to end up with it, and when one of those dreaded rats stuck its head through the roof and peered into your bunk, it wasn't pleasant. Pass the bayonet . . .

8

TOOLS OF THE TRADE

I WAS PROUD TO FIGHT with the Black Watch, the finest regiment in the land. I was honoured to serve the British Army. I was humbled to go into battle with some of the most dedicated men I have ever met.

It is unfortunate that the best regiment, best force and best individuals did not receive the very best when it came to kit. Quite frankly, we were like the poor cousins out there in Korea among our allies – not least when we stood shoulder to shoulder with the Americans. They were, it is fair to say, streets ahead of us when it came to uniform and weaponry.

It did not take long for us to appreciate how far behind we lagged; in truth, that started to become apparent even before we had completed our training. It was while we were in Inverness that we got to know the quirks of the weapons that would become the tools of our trade.

On the line in Korea, we were left horribly exposed by our kit. We were still firing bolt-action rifles while the Yanks had semi-automatics with five bullets for a single pull of the trigger. The old bolt-action offerings, which had been around in the First World War and even long before that with little change, were fine for hunting and sport – but in a combat situation they were obviously much slower and more cumbersome to use than the more modern equivalents. The difference was like night and day, which is not ideal when it really is a matter of life and death.

Aside from those rifles, we also had our Sten guns. Those wee sub-machine guns would have been great if it wasn't for one thing: they never worked properly. The springs were rubbish, and you just couldn't rely on them to fire when you wanted them to and couldn't bet on them not firing when you didn't want them to. It was a nightmare.

Millions of them were churned out in and around the Second World War and the Korean War – they were cheap to make in large volumes – and amazingly they were still being used into the 1960s. I don't think too many tears would have been shed in any of the regiments when the Sten was phased out. It was a weapon with a reputation for being unreliable and was at the root of countless accidents at home and abroad.

There were signs that the message was getting through during my service. Every effort was made to improve the situation and get to grips with the problem. It appeared as though the top brass were looking at what was available to other forces and trying to bring us in line with that, thankfully. It wasn't in their interests to send out troops who weren't able to do their jobs properly.

They still talk now about kit not being up to scratch and my heart goes out to any soldier posted into combat without the gear to do the job, although I understand that in recent years big strides have been made in ensuring our boys in Afghanistan and other far-flung locations have the gear to suit their surroundings.

The Sten was a case in point, notorious for not being great in hot conditions. Mind you, it wasn't great in any weather. We were trained to take it to pieces after every patrol, re-oil the moving parts and generally treat it like our life depended on it, which it did, unfortunately. If the first clip didn't fire, you'd grab another one; if that one didn't fire, it was time to look for your rifle – a complete disaster.

The episode I would look back to came during a night patrol. I had spent hours taking my Sten to pieces, cleaning every part, oiling it, greasing it and painstakingly putting it back together the way we had been trained to. When you went out on patrol in the paddy, you would always give your weapon a blast into a pit that had been dug for that very purpose – just to make sure everything was in order before going out on point. So I did just that with my shiny, lovingly cleaned Sten – and the bloody thing was perfectly still and worryingly quiet. Not even a cough or splutter – it was jammed solid.

Imagine going out into no-man's-land with one of those things. It makes me shudder just thinking about it. At the back of your mind was always the thought that the thing would let you down.

During my time in Korea, a replacement for the Sten was being considered. It was the Sterling sub-machine gun, which I believe came into play after the Sten, and I did get the chance to test one on the line. It was a damn sight better than its predecessor. I could tell that almost as soon as I lifted it for the first time and pulled the trigger. For a start, it actually fired. The Sterling remained the British Army's machine gun of choice for the next three decades, so I clearly wasn't alone in my assessment of its performance. Unfortunately, no sooner had I been handed one than it was taken back again. We only had them on trial, so it was back to the less than trusty old Sten.

It wasn't just our arms that were out of kilter with what the Americans had; even our clothing wasn't quite up to scratch. That may sound like a minor grumble, but when you understand the conditions we were facing, you get a better idea of why it really mattered to us.

I cast my mind back to my first day out on the line, following hard on the heels of my first night in a hooch. I'd had hardly any sleep, as a result of the adrenalin from being moved forward and of the nervous anticipation of what lay ahead – that and the freezing cold we were exposed to. The hooch at least gave a little protection from the elements, but once we moved out in the morning we were hit with the most incredible frost. Us Scots may think we've seen it all when it comes to inclement weather, but this took my breath away, quite literally.

I had my scarf pulled round my mouth – the rules made it clear you couldn't cover your ears – as we trooped towards the forward trench, but the vapour from my warm breath in the bitterly cold air was being pushed upwards and was freezing in clumps on my eyelashes. If I closed my eyes for a second or two, the lashes would freeze together. It was like nothing I have experienced before or since, even in the harshest of Highland winters.

There was occasional snow, but that wasn't the problem. It was the hard, hard frosts and bone-chilling temperatures that hit us hardest. In winter in north Asia, arctic winds sweep across from Siberia. There was little we could do about it, and out on the line or lying still on the floor of a trench it was far from fun. There were incidents of frostbite and the like, with the cold penetrating the gear we wore.

We were allowed gloves, but of course you had to take them off to rub your eyes and brush away the ice. That, coupled with the sleep deprivation that inevitably came with life on the line, made it a very uncomfortable existence in our bog-standard woolly jumpers, combat jackets and trousers. Then there were the vests, heavy string vests. They were designed to offer a bit of protection, but it wasn't exactly hi-tech stuff.

Now, the Americans, on the other hand, arrived ready for the worst the Korean winter could throw at them. They wore shiny new parka jackets, zipped up to the eyeballs and keeping them nice and cosy. They were so nice, in fact, that some of our boys managed to 'acquire' one or two of them. I don't know for sure how they all came by them, but I do know that some of the jackets were gifted by the Yanks. They could see we were up against it, and when the high-ranking American officers came to visit us, they would quite often bring a handful of jackets to give out to the lucky few. I'm afraid I wasn't among the winners in the great kit lottery, so I had to make do with layering myself up as best I could.

What I did manage to do was borrow one of those elusive parkas for the occasional patrol, and what a difference it made. They were mohair-lined and wonderfully warm, with a little tail that dropped down the back and fastened through your legs. It was like wearing a sleeping bag, it was that cosy. I'm told you can still buy them today, the old fishtail parkas. They're still made using the finest materials, just as they were back then, with a cotton and nylon shell for bouncing the rain off and that heavy mohair liner. While we were scrambling around to get our hands on one to share between us, every US man was kitted out with one, as they shipped hundreds of thousands of them out there.

The chiefs did what they could to give us what we needed. We got a survival pack, complete with water-sterilising tablets, clasp knives, safety pins, and bits and pieces that we could barter with – cigarette lighters, things like that – if we got in a sticky position. While we felt under-equipped, I wouldn't criticise the British Army chiefs too strongly. The Korean War was like no other, and certainly the climate caught everyone by surprise. I can only imagine they were caught on the hop a little bit.

9

WORK, REST AND PLAY

TO PAINT OUR TIME IN Korea as all work and no play would be wrong. There were lighter moments to lift the spirits amid the gloomier times, and for me the release came through a familiar and welcome pursuit: football. You can take the men out of Scotland, but you can't take Scotland out of the men!

As a schoolboy, I had blossomed into something of a player. I had gone through youth football and YMCA leagues and had progressed into the man's world of the junior game, one level below the professionals in Scotland. Then, not long before I'd been recruited by the Black Watch, I'd been given my break in senior football by East Fife. I'd looked all set to carve out a career for myself in the sport when the Army came calling.

Never in my wildest dreams had I pictured myself playing in front of a crowd under the Korean sun, but that was exactly what happened. Thousands of miles from home, far from the playing fields we all grew up kicking a ball around on, they had cleared an area back at camp and created a brilliant full-size football pitch. There was an embankment behind one of the goals, like a makeshift stand, perfect for watching the games from.

There were a good few bounce games on that patch of ground, but its main purpose was to play host to the real action: the inter-battalion tournament. Having played in senior football, albeit fleetingly, I was in the thick of it. They'd known before I'd gone out there that I had a football background, and obviously that had been noted. It wasn't as though there were trial games as such. It was well organised, though, with a very handy team put together and some decent players involved. The standard was impressive, especially when you consider that many of us were battle-weary by that point. It's amazing how quickly you forget fatigue when there's a ball to be won, though!

My involvement meant that I was pulled back from the line, along with the rest of the side, to prepare for the matches and then play in them. The games were the talk of the camp and drew a lot of interest from the boys, with the standard pretty high and a real competitive edge to the matches. We might have been fighting as one force, but there were a few battles between the battalions on the football pitch!

We did well, going on to win the competition and take the glory . . . as well as the trappings of success. For us, that meant a celebration in the officers' mess and the rare chance for a few refreshments.

All the boys were winding me up before I went, telling me that I had to remember them and take them back a dram or two. Well, the night wore on and the party was in full swing. The drink was flowing and everyone was in good spirits, including me. After all, it would have been rude not to join in!

But, even in my, shall we say, 'relaxed' state, I did remember my pals back in our living quarters. I found an empty pint pot and did the rounds of the mess, blagging nips from the officers. Instead of drinking them myself, I'd pour them into this pint pot when they weren't looking, filling it to the brim before making my excuses and swaying my way back to camp.

I don't remember too much after that; it's fair to say I slept well after my nightcaps. When I woke the next morning, I was getting a real roasting from the lads. They were giving me a torrid time, goading me for not bringing them back a drink. It didn't matter how much I protested that I had, they were having none of it.

Eventually, they cracked, though, and told me they did believe my story about the overflowing pint pot. Not that they'd seen any of the whisky, mind you. Apparently I'd come marauding through the tent door in the early hours, full of the joys, proudly clutching a handle – nothing else. What became of the rest of it, we'll never know!

The well-lubricated celebration in the post-football haze was one of the perks of my dual trade as soldier and footballer, with the latter providing me with chances that others in our ranks might have grasped with both hands. Perhaps the most notable opportunity my sporting talents presented to me was the option of not going on front-line duty at all. I rejected that straight away, but the fact that I was given the choice is a demonstration of the benefits that went hand in hand with a football background.

Through all my exploits in Korea, good times and bad, at the back of my mind was the fact I didn't have to be there at all. I had got a couple of offers of not going in the first place – purely down to football, nothing else. Word had got around that there was a senior player in the ranks, and there was pressure from above to try to keep me on home soil, obviously with the army football team in mind.

First, they offered me a place in parachute training, which would have meant I could have avoided going out on active duty and stayed at home to learn that particular trade. First things first, I didn't much fancy the prospect of chucking myself out of a plane at 20,000 feet. I might have been pretty fearless, but that was one thing that didn't particularly fill me with enthusiasm.

When they realised the parachute plan was a no-go, the next offer was of staying at home as a physical-training instructor. They told me I could still do my bit in PT but avoid having to stray too far from home and steer clear of the front line. As attractive as they tried to make it sound, it just wasn't for me. The rest of the men I had trained with were all going into battle and it didn't cross my mind for a second that I wouldn't be going with them.

I don't think I would ever have forgiven myself if I had taken the easy way out; it would have been on my conscience for the rest of my days. We had joined together, learned the ropes together and would fight together. There was no way I would be persuaded otherwise. The others didn't have a choice and I didn't see why I should either.

It wasn't just about loyalty to those I served with. I would be lying if I tried to claim it was. The other big factor was that I had a real sense of adventure. I knew there was a big world out there and I wanted to see it for myself, the nice and the nasty. It turned out that I certainly got my wish on that score.

We really didn't know much about what was waiting for us in Korea. The world was a bigger place then; there was no Internet or 24-hour television news to beam pictures of the fighting back home. Of course, we'd hear snippets here and there from people who had been out there, or we'd read accounts in the papers, but nothing in great detail.

We relied on word of mouth and the occasional pearl of wisdom from those who had been out on duty. There were some who served in Korea who came away with a chip on their shoulder. They could never understand why they had been there, wondering why they had been sent to fight a war so far from home and so far from what they saw as relevant to them. Others took it in their stride and were enthusiastic about what we faced.

What I would always say is that if you could have the experience that I and my fellow soldiers in the Black Watch had, you would say it was the greatest thing in the world. Of course, you have to be lucky to get through and out in one piece, and I consider that

I was: lucky to survive, lucky to be able to look back more than 50 years on and remember what it was like out there and lucky to have served with a wonderful regiment.

For me, the welcome release of football in Korea was the best of times followed quickly by the worst of times. Very soon after I'd had that rush of lifting the trophy with my teammates, we were jolted back to reality as we were shepherded into the Bren gun carriers and shuttled away to return to a stormy scene on the line.

Just days after celebrating back at camp, I found myself lying in a lonely part of the battlefield riddled with bullets and not knowing whether I'd live to see another day. Whether I'd play another game was the furthest thing from my mind; the main aim was to get through another day.

10

THE LONG ROAD TO RECOVERY

WHEN I WOKE IN THE field-hospital bed in Korea, my first reaction was one of fear when I heard the shells and artillery in the distance. The second was one of relief. I was in a bad way, of that there was no doubt, but I was alive. What gradually began to dawn on me, as I spoke to the doctors and took in what was going on all around me, was that I was far from out of the woods.

I'd been shot up pretty badly and wounded seriously in many places. The fact that I survived was partly down to good fortune and largely down to the early intervention of the American medics who first got their hands on me and stabilised my condition so expertly, ensuring I survived in those crucial first few hours.

That care continued in the field hospital, where, alongside men of all nationalities who had suffered in similar fashions, I was tended to day and night. Those early days were about cleaning me up and doing a patching-up job, making sure infection didn't set in and that the bleeding had been stemmed.

It was the first stage of a long and painful road that would see me treated in four countries on two continents. The next part of my journey took me the short distance from our base in Korea to

Japan and the military hospital in Kure, or the British Commonwealth General Hospital, to give it its Sunday name.

It had been in existence for well over half a century when I checked in, and was complete with a casualty department, a surgery section and specialist wards covering everything from orthopaedics to dermatology, in a maze of corridors and wings spanning several storeys. There were hundreds of beds in the sprawling old building, with British medics working alongside those from Australia and Canada to look after us. I believe the place had originally been built in the nineteenth century as a naval hospital, but it had developed to become a centre for all of the forces. I'm told it's still standing today, serving the Japanese people as a general hospital.

I have to say the facilities for treating the wounded soldiers were good, even if there were a few teething problems (more on that soon). I felt I was in a safe place, and being removed from the fighting allowed me to concentrate on my recovery, channelling all my energy into getting myself better as quickly as I could. It was reassuring to be in a place that was geared solely towards that and well equipped to cater for the various battlefield injuries the medical staff had to contend with.

In my days at Kure, there were so many good and dedicated people, experts in every field imaginable, having to cope with the most trying of circumstances. The cases they had to deal with on a daily basis must have been haunting, but they never flinched.

The hospital should have been a place of sanctuary, and in the main it was – save for a few experiences that will live with me forever and ever. For one thing, the terrible injuries of the men all around me could not do anything other than have a deep impact. I was badly wounded, but I could see there were many in worse positions. You could not take comfort from that, but it gave you a sense of perspective.

The lad in the next bed to me was a fellow Scot. He had had

both of his legs blown off. His story was a terrifying one. A shell had landed in front of him on the line and the blast from it had knocked a box of grenades into his gun pit. He had frantically tried to get out before they went off, but his legs were still dangling over the edge when the whole box exploded, taking his legs off.

We struck up a friendship as we came to terms with our injuries in Kure, trying our best to keep each other's spirits up. That was not always possible, however, and he went through a terrible ordeal while on the ward.

One morning, I woke to hear him screaming his head off. I shouted for a nurse to come and help, and she came running through, ripping the sheets off his bed before throwing them to the floor. The source of the terror was clear. During the night, a plague of red ants had invaded the ward. It wasn't unusual, but on this occasion the usual precautions hadn't been taken. What they did was put all four legs of the bed into big pots of butter, so the ants couldn't climb them. They also made sure that no bedclothes were trailing on the floor, so there was no way up.

That night, though, his sheets had been hanging down, and the ants had found their path. They'd crawled up in their thousands and made straight for the flesh where his legs had been amputated. He was traumatised, not surprisingly, and to watch his suffering was horrendous. Can you imagine going through the pain of losing your legs and then waking to find you're crawling with ants? It makes me shudder just thinking about it.

I'd been flown into Japan by plane from the battlefield in Korea, and that little episode with the ant colony took place just a few hours after I'd arrived. It was a more dramatic introduction than I would have hoped for, and such incidents kept on coming. Not too long after I was admitted, I went through my second major scare during my time in Kure when we were hit by an earthquake.

The whole place was plunged into turmoil, with the vibrations and tremors strong enough to move the furniture around. My own bed was shunted 30 yards across the ward and, once again, the helplessness of your own situation hits you as you realise there's nothing at all you can do, except lie there and wait to see what happens.

To be fair, the Japanese were well prepared for earthquakes and the building had been constructed with that in mind, so the damage was minimal. It was more the fright that got us. We managed to ride out that particular storm – pretty small beer in comparison with what I and so many of my fellow patients had experienced back in Korea.

Two or three guys came in with very bad injuries, and it was a strange thing to realise when you talked to them that they had lost their spirit, given up. It wasn't something that had ever entered my mind. I was determined to fight; from the minute I fell in the field, I was adamant that I wouldn't be beaten by my injuries. Some people went the other way.

My man with the ants, in the bed opposite, was a toughie, though. He was determined he was going to do something with his life. I'm sad to say I've no idea what became of him, but I would bet my last pound that he made a go of it. I certainly hope he did.

My own mindset was very similar. I was in a position that wasn't great, but I would persevere. The Yanks had given me a tube in my bladder, connected to a pump, and another tube and pump for my bowels. It was far from ideal, obviously, but it was a solution. There were accidents along the way, including one occasion when the pump for my bladder got choked and there was a real panic among the nursing team. In the middle of the night, I was swelling up like a balloon, in a lot of pain. They tried to get a doctor and couldn't, until eventually somebody rushed in to deal with it. I was in a mess, but it was just a minor setback in the scheme of things.

I had three operations in Japan, and it was very much a case of trying to be patient, letting the medics do their work and allowing my body to heal itself as best it could. I was under chloroform a number of times, really not aware of what was going on around me.

They decided one day, after three or four weeks, to address the bladder problem, believing it had healed enough to allow normal function. They had been working on various things for weeks and decided that the pump I was hooked up to could go. It was a big occasion, with all the relevant doctors and nurses gathered around as I prepared to go for a pee. They got me sitting up in bed and handed me a glass bottle. This was it, the start of my recovery. Normal life. I'd been drinking plenty of fluids all day and they ran the tap to fill the room with the sound of running water. There was jubilation when I said, 'That's it! It's going great!'

The relief I felt was brilliant: such a little thing to be able to go to the toilet normally, but such a major thing for me. Then I started to feel a little bit wet where I was sitting. I thought I must have missed the bottle, so I lifted the sheet to adjust it – then realised there wasn't a drop in it. It turned out the pee was coming out of my backside. From such joy, it was back to the realisation that there wasn't going to be anything easy about the road to health.

So it was back to the pump, back to square one. The sister on my ward was a woman from Stornoway, an absolute gem of a lady. She saw me through a lot of bad times, and the day after the trial-and-error session she came to me and said she thought I might just qualify for *The Guinness Book of Records*: my little trick with the empty bottle was certainly a first as far as she was concerned. A bit of gallows humour helped to lighten things up when they got too dark.

That lady from the Isles was the highlight of the hospital for me, from an emotional point of view. She worked wonders to care for our minds as well as our injuries. In later years, after my family had moved up to the Highlands and settled in Gairloch, I got a note to say the sister was back home in Stornoway. It was a very busy time, with Vi and me in the middle of building our hotel, and by the time I eventually made it to Lewis she had died. It's a cause of regret, because I arrived at Kure suffering from a lot of bad wounds and her efforts in caring for me and keeping my spirits up were so important. I wish I'd been able to meet her one last time and thank her for what she had done all those years before.

In Japan, I went through two or three operations to try to help out, but there was nothing they could do with my drainage problems. That was the end of it for me, in Asia at least. They had done what they could, and, having been deemed fit enough to travel, I was sent on my way.

First stop was Singapore, then on to Malta and then home. Everything went pretty well with the transfer, save for a slight issue coming into Malta. The plane we were in was hit with a spot of mechanical trouble, and it took a couple of days to get it patched up and ready to go back to the UK. The nursing staff prepped me for the journey again and we took off, me and another passenger as the only stretcher cases – and, even before we got going, he was more than a touch hysterical about the prospect of the flight. We took off and when we hit what must have been around 25,000 feet an attendant came to talk to us. He said, 'Don't be distressed, but we have to check on the stalling speed – it's just part of the preparations to make sure everything's safe for coming in to land.'

I remember thinking to myself, 'Oh God, is there no end to this?'

Before we knew it, we were plummeting nose down towards the ground. We probably dropped 10,000 feet all in all, and it felt like a long way down, with the nagging doubt that we wouldn't be coming back up again. I can't begin to tell you how glad I was to hear those engines cough and splutter back into life. I was a physical and mental wreck when we landed back in Britain.

We were taken to Aldershot and I went through what was becoming a familiar process of trial and error with the medical teams at the army base there.

It said a lot that I could say to myself, 'I was lucky.' Some of the cases in the other beds were burns victims, mostly victims of napalm and shelling injuries. Because they were moaning and screaming in pain, they were segregated from the rest of us more often than not, but you couldn't help but be aware of how gruesome some of the wounds were.

The next stage was more messing around with me – a series of minor operations that didn't succeed in doing anything that was a major step forward. They therefore sent me to the Queen Alexandra's Military Hospital at Millbank in London, on the banks of the Thames. Nowadays, the site is home to part of the Tate Britain art gallery and museum complex and the Chelsea College of Art and Design, but back then it was a hive of services activity. It was a hospital as well as a training centre for medics, having opened in 1905 and quickly grown.

Millbank eventually closed in 1977 – a crying shame given the sterling work that was done there. It was a huge facility filled with RAF, army and navy personnel. That big old hospital would change my life, or at least the senior surgeon would. He was a gentleman by the name of Colonel Hunt.

I owe so much to that man. He was a surgeon of all sorts, but he specialised in skin grafts and was skilled in working on stomach problems. He was clearly a man of vast intelligence, but he was also a man who had the willingness to use that for the benefit of others. The consensus around the hospital was that he was very much ahead of his time with the way he went about his business, and his record of getting men back into service spoke volumes. After all, that was what the army medics were there for: to make sure as few men as possible were invalided out of the forces.

By the time he was finished with me, after a number of weeks and a number of operations, I was near enough a new man. For a start, he had my bladder functioning as normal and my back passage working without a colostomy – although not particularly well.

In fact, he said to me, 'I see you were a footballer.' I objected strongly to the word 'were', much to his amusement. He said, 'You're not seriously thinking of going back to it?' I told him I was, I would give it a go, and he retorted, 'I'll give you a tip: if you get fast enough to get in front of someone on the football field, they'll never catch you – they'll be too busy slipping behind on what's coming out of you.' Charming, I thought, but I knew he was doing everything he could to get me back to health. Perhaps not aiming for match fit, right enough, but well enough to live a normal life at least.

He worked away and worked away on me, surgery after surgery, and gradually chipped away at all of the problems and all of the wounds I had been left with. I still bear the scars today, but that's a small price to pay.

From the day I got hit to the day I walked out of the door of the hospital in London, it was 12 months, a whole year of my life lost, but I had so much to be thankful for and Colonel Hunt was at the centre of that.

In my darkest hour in Korea, when I was dragging myself through the trenches looking for help, I hadn't dared to think about the future. For months, in fact, I probably hadn't wanted to look forward, not knowing what the years ahead might hold.

As the doors of Millbank closed behind me, I was able to be confident for the first time that the worst was behind me and that

TOUGHER THAN BULLETS

I was ready to start moving forward with my life. I was still far from back to normal, with a lot of hard work and treatment still to come, but I walked out of that building full of spirit and ready for the next stage.

11

THE HOMECOMING

HAVING BEEN TO KOREA, JAPAN, Malta (albeit briefly) and England, it was time to come home. I had set off hoping to see the world and satisfy my hunger for adventure. In the end, I got far more than I bargained for on my travels, and when the opportunity arose to return to Scotland I didn't need a second invitation.

From London, I was transported north to begin the next stage of my recovery, and my destination was the Bridge of Earn rehabilitation hospital. The Army had booked me in there to complete the excellent work that had been done by Colonel Hunt and his team at Millbank.

I didn't have a choice; it was all decided for me. Anyway, what would I have done otherwise? Walked away from the army at that stage, gone back to civilian life and made do with the physical state I'd been left in? It wasn't an attractive proposition. With the hospital near enough to home – Perth was just three miles away – it was a chance to be back on familiar territory and to work away on my rehab in an environment that was as good as any.

I ended up spending exactly two years and sixty-six days in the army. That's sixty-six days longer than my national service should have been. All that, and not a penny extra! Still, at least

I got the chance to spend the second half of that time back on home soil.

Bridge of Earn Hospital had opened in 1940, one of the many established, from Selkirk in the south to Inverness in the north, for the Second World War effort and with space for more than 1,000 men. It had taken patients from all over, including casualties from the bombing raids on London and even the Normandy invasion. Prisoners of war were treated too, and for years Bridge of Earn had been a busy, busy place.

When the war ended, the focus changed to rehabilitation, and a unit that had been housed at the Gleneagles Hotel was transferred to Bridge of Earn. An orthopaedic unit that had been housed at Larbert also shifted up there in 1947, meaning that the hospital survived for decades. It wasn't until the early 1990s that it closed for good. I think the site is now earmarked for housing.

It will make a nice spot to live, surrounded by the rolling countryside of Perthshire. The tranquil setting was one of the factors that made it ideal as a rehabilitation centre. It was far from the hustle and bustle of the city, with no distractions. The men who were there could concentrate solely on getting well; they had the peace and quiet to focus their minds and regroup.

I spent pretty much another year at Bridge of Earn, a punishing year at that, and I am so glad that I did. The other choice would have been to give up and live out my life as a cripple. I was told in no uncertain terms that if I didn't do the work and follow the rehab plans in front of me, no matter how painful it was or how tired my body was, the consequences would be severe. You have the opportunity immediately after being injured to try to put things right. You can't go back 30 years later and do it; by then, it's too late and the damage cannot be undone.

People have described me as 'tough'. I tell you this, it was never about being tough or hard. It was all about looking after myself, self-preservation. I had my life in front of me and knew nobody owed me a living. I had to get myself fit and stand on my own two feet in every sense.

From the moment the first bullet hit my body, I knew what I had to do. As soon as it happens, self-preservation kicks in: 'What can I do to get myself out of this?' In my case, I stumbled out of the line of fire. It was dark, there was nobody else around, it was down to me to get myself to safety. If that desire is strong enough, you'll do it; if not, you will end up dead. I could have lain there where I had been hit, waiting to be saved, but I could have been there a long time. With confusion all around, I couldn't expect a rescue party, so I dragged myself up and did what I had to.

It shouldn't be overlooked that many people helped me along the way, and I certainly couldn't have got back on my feet on my own. There were the first American medics who picked me up in Korea, the staff in the hospital in Japan, and then Colonel Hunt and his team in London. Then there were those at Bridge of Earn – led by a certain Davie Kinnear.

Football fans will know Davie for his service to Rangers, but at the hospital it was his physiotherapy skills that earned him his reputation. He took me under his wing, giving me extra treatment and rehab to push me along the way. I was still on the books of East Fife at that stage, as Davie knew, and in hindsight I probably got better treatment than most because we struck up a strong bond. He could still be fearsome, though, and gave me some real beastings, with the best of intentions.

I worked hard – he knew I would – and he responded by building me up to the point where I was stronger, faster and fitter than ever before. Davie was a top, top man. He had to stay within the limits of what was allowed at the hospital, but he took it right to the limit.

Before I arrived at the hospital and became one of his patients, I was well aware of Davie and his reputation as a very fine football player. He was a fellow Fifer and had cut his teeth with Raith

Rovers before joining Rangers in the 1930s, going on to make more than a century of appearances in a light-blue jersey. If it hadn't been for the outbreak of the Second World War, he would have made a great deal more, no doubt, but he was one of many Ibrox men who put football to one side to join the cause. In peacetime, he went on to play for Third Lanark and Dunfermline before concentrating on his work as a physiotherapist in the hospitals, and it was there that our paths crossed for the first time.

It was a long, long road from the start line in Korea to the finish in Perth, and it wasn't an easy path. It was spread over more than two years and I saw the inside of more surgical theatres than I care to remember, but we got there.

It wasn't without its hurdles, and even by the time I reached Bridge of Earn it wasn't exactly plain sailing. I've become used to finding people trying to knock me down a peg or two, and it was no different when I was flat on my back and trying desperately to get myself fit again. At the hospital, Davie had a colleague who was a bit of a macho man and took a dislike to me for whatever reason. I don't recall ever giving him reason to take umbrage, but he was not a fan and that was clear for all to see.

Davie would leave me in his hands, telling him to put me through this course or that. In reality, what happened was that this character would make me do things that he knew I shouldn't be doing and hope I'd fall flat on my face – quite literally. Either that or he'd be trying to drop medicine balls on my stomach, knowing fine well the injuries I had and the damage that could potentially be done.

One day, he appeared and said, 'You'll have to go into the examination room.' I said, 'Sure thing,' not thinking anything of it. I went along and, as was normal procedure for examinations, got undressed, got on the bed, pulled the big towel over me to protect my modesty and lay back.

The door burst open and it was my man: 'Right, we've got some apprentices here, interested in war wounds.' Trooping after him was a crew of girls, all physiotherapy students whom I recognised from seeing them on their placement at the hospital. The bastard was at it; this little examination was all for his benefit.

He said, 'Right, ladies, this is a victim of the Korean War.' With that, he whipped my towel off and left me sitting there in front of the assembled audience in nothing but my birthday suit.

I was absolutely fizzing and the girls were giggling because they could see my reaction. I had to think fast. So I just sat there, bold as brass, and smiled. The whole thing had been turned on its head, and the architect-in-chief was none too happy. He wasn't finding it funny at all.

I had to put up with weeks of that clown's antics. If I'd been in any place else, I would have clobbered him, but it was still a military facility and I prided myself on my discipline when I was on active service. I wasn't going to let that slip now I was back home. Besides, he was just a side issue; my main focus was getting back on my feet. Day in and day out, I went through the mill, and after months of gruelling work I was getting there, getting stronger every day.

When I'd gone through my operations in Japan and London, I'd been bedridden, but I'd been able to get gingerly back on my feet before I left the bright lights of the city. The damage that had been done to my right foot when I'd been shot was the main barrier to me walking. The bullet wound itself caused discomfort and there was a nick on the instep, too. The bigger problem, though, was the shattered heel bone, which took time to mend. In a sense, I got off lightly with that, though. If the bullet had been an inch higher, it would have gone straight through my Achilles tendon, and I don't imagine that would have been easy to fix.

In fact, I know it wouldn't have been. Many years later, fairly recently, in fact, I fell from a ladder at home and snapped the tendon in the same ankle, and the pain was incredible. We were heading off on holiday soon after and the prospect of going away with one foot in plaster didn't appeal, so I braved it out and left it untreated. That was a mistake, as I'm still troubled by it to this day – just another mishap to add to the list.

I've lost count of the number of scars I have on my body. It's far in excess of 20 and not all of them can be blamed on the Army. From the chunk that was taken out of my ear when I was hit with a bottle as a youngster to the split on my nose from my brief boxing career at the YMCA in Perth, I've put my flesh and bones through some punishment over the years.

Naturally, I still bear the scars from my operations in the military hospital in London; my stomach's a bit of a patchwork. But the main thing was that the procedures had the desired effect, and by the time I arrived at Bridge of Earn I was back on my own two feet and ready to get to work. The hospital was surrounded by open countryside, but rather than admiring the views I spent the bulk of my time staring at four walls.

The majority of my work was done inside in the gym, where I started by building up from walking to a light jog and then on to proper running. Each stage was another milestone, even if I was still a fair bit away from kicking a ball.

The other main strand of the rehab was building up my muscles again after the various dents my body had suffered. For a start, the abdominal surgery I'd had repeatedly to try to sort out my stomach had meant the surgeons cutting through my stomach muscles time and time again. That had to be addressed and the only way to do so was slowly and steadily, with plenty of repetition to regain the strength I had once had. They were hard times but good times. That was because I knew what the end goal was: getting back out on a football pitch, wherever that might be. It didn't matter whether it was Ibrox or the local park. I simply wanted to prove to myself, not to anyone else, that I could get back to the physical level I had been at before I went off to war.

My legs, my arms ... everything had to be worked again and again. It got to the stage where I could start to lift weights as part of my daily routine and in time I felt comfortable in my own body once more. I didn't fully recover – I never have – and I always had to be careful about what I put myself through. I had to find my own limits when it came to training. I certainly couldn't rattle off a hundred sit-ups, but I could still do the same as most men and more than many.

Eventually, Davie Kinnear took a look at me being put through my paces in the gym and pulled me aside to tell me he thought I was ready to play a game of football, if I fancied it. That was music to my ears. I trusted his judgement and if he thought I was up to it then I was.

It went from there. I turned out in a few games for Newburgh juniors while continuing to knock my pan in during the rehab sessions. Davie had played alongside Scot Symon at Rangers and, with Mr Symon back at Ibrox as manager, stayed in touch. Davie must have given me a good review, because before long I had the opportunity to move to Ibrox.

The manager – who, by coincidence, had been my boss at East Fife before my army service – knew me and liked me as a player, but I have absolutely no doubt that I owe Davie Kinnear a huge debt of gratitude.

Just a few years after our time together at Bridge of Earn, he returned to Rangers full time as part of Mr Symon's backroom team and we were reunited. He would take training in the mornings and work in the treatment room in the afternoons. In both roles, he gave wonderful service.

His death, in 2008, was greeted with tremendous sadness by everyone with a connection to Rangers. He had a great football brain, he was an excellent physiotherapist and, above all else, he was a wonderful man, to whom I owe an awful lot.

12

IN THE BEGINNING

I'M A FIFER BORN AND bred, but part of my heart will always be in Perth. Although my early years were spent in Fife, in many ways the biggest events in my life all followed our move as a family across to the heart of the country. It was there that I signed up for the Army, it was there that I convalesced after service and it was there that the seeds of my career in sport were sown.

Who knows what course my life would have followed had we remained where the family's roots were, or what stories I might have had to tell? What I do know is that life certainly turned out to be far from predictable for me and those closest to me. The twists and turns I went through growing up made me the man I became, and the unexpected events of my adult life have shaped the person I am today. Experiences big and small are all locked away in the memory bank.

I count myself very fortunate. I have been able to live three lives, very different but all rewarding and exhilarating in their own way.

As a soldier, I was able to travel the world and serve my country, to take to the high seas and set foot on foreign shores, to see things, good and bad, that I would never have expected. I served shoulder to shoulder with some wonderful men and experienced the type of camaraderie that can be found only on the battlefield. Many did not return to reflect on those experiences and I will never forget those who did not.

As a sportsman, I also visited countries and places that would have been beyond my wildest dreams as a young boy making his way in the world. Playing for a club as well organised and well heeled as Rangers, we received the very best treatment and moved in circles with the great and good both inside and outside of football. It was a privileged existence, and I always appreciated that and the benefits it brought me.

As a lover of our wonderful country, I have been fortunate to have lived in a wild and untouched corner of the land for decades now. My wife and I settled in the West Highland village of Gairloch as we embarked on a new career in the hospitality trade, not only allowing us to find our way in business but enabling me to indulge my passion for fishing in some of the most dramatic and enchanting surroundings any angler could wish for. Now, in retirement, I continue to embrace the lifestyle we are so fortunate to enjoy in a place I consider to be our own little paradise.

Three very different chapters in my life, but each with their own vivid memories and reasons for me to be thankful for my lot. Different twists and turns at various junctures could have taken me down other routes, but I've picked out the right path for me.

I tried never to lose sight of my roots or to get carried away with the success I enjoyed in football. Having seen the realities of war at first hand, there was always a reference point to put sport in its rightful context.

That isn't to say I took the game more lightly than any other person who pulled on a jersey on a Saturday afternoon – I hope anyone who saw me play would testify to that. I would always fight for my team and teammates. That was deep in my nature, and that spirit carried me a long way. I hope that, as a soldier and a football player, I was a man who could be relied upon whatever the circumstances, and the skills and qualities required in the two arenas tended to complement each other. Whether the characteristics that I still have to this day were with me from the day I was born or instilled in me, I'm not so sure. I like to think it was a bit of both.

It was in the Fife town of Cupar that I came into the world, born on 10 May in 1933. I was one of four children, growing up with my elder sisters Cathleen and Marion and my younger brother Frank – the rogue of the family. My formative years were spent in the Kingdom, before we left for Perth at the end of the Second World War, and the family's ties to the east coast stretched right back for generations.

My father worked in the beet factory just outside Cupar. The factory had been set up in the 1920s, the only one of its type in Scotland, and it stayed open right through to 1972. An industrial estate was later built on the site, but my memories are all of the factory at its peak, when it was right at the heart of the community, giving work to so many men and putting food on so many tables. It was probably taken for granted at the time, but it was such an important part of life in the area.

Cupar was Fife's main market town at that time and sugar beet became an important crop. The juice would be squeezed from the beets and sent to the boiler as part of the sugar-making process. It was still a relatively new industry for the area when I was growing up, but it took off quickly and Cupar was a vibrant enough town, buoyed by the activity at the factory and the employment it provided.

It was hard manual work, with the men putting in long hours, but my father made enough to be able to put some money aside from his wages as well as keeping the family going. He obviously had a plan in mind, and in time he was able to put it into action, taking us away from Fife for a new life when I was still a young boy. His savings from his wages, along with the prize funds he made from boxing at the fairs and some money he was able to borrow from his brothers, allowed him to get out of the factory and buy a pub in Perth.

While he was in Cupar during the Second World War, he was excused from army duty because he had problems with stomach ulcers, although he did serve in the home guard. That entailed learning how to disable explosive devices, as well as how to use the 'sticky bombs' that had been developed. These bombs came about after it became clear that bullets simply wouldn't penetrate enemy tanks; even hand grenades would just bounce off them. In response, a 2-lb explosive that could be stuck to the turret of a tank or even to a pillbox at close quarters was designed, but it wasn't without its pitfalls, as we found out.

One day, during an exercise in using sticky bombs, my dad was unlucky enough to have one of the bombs stick to his hand and it exploded while he was holding it, blowing three of his fingers off. As you can imagine, it was a big scare for us all and he was fortunate to survive, given the damage the bombs were designed to do to tanks and other armoury. It was a reminder, as if we needed one, that the war was very real and very dangerous.

Like so many families, we had an Anderson shelter at the bottom of the garden, and we had to scamper down there to take cover from a few of the night bombing raids that the Germans launched on Fife. With the Leuchars air base not too far away, we were very much on their radar. Leuchars had been a training base until the war, then it became active, with planes from the base becoming the first British aircraft to engage with the enemy. Because of that, it was only natural that the area was on a heightened alert throughout the war.

We heard the explosions on occasion, and felt the sand raining down from the ceiling of the shelter when the bombs fell close by, but we were generally well shielded from the full horrors of the time. Of course, we knew what was happening and read or listened to the reports coming back from the front line, but life carried on as best it could. That was my first experience of war, and it clearly did nothing to put me off the army life. The sense of adventure I'd always had ensured there was something appealing about the forces to me.

I was a typical boy's boy and got into a few scrapes, most of them my own doing. I knew that if I stepped out of line I'd be in trouble at home, but it didn't always stop me from getting into hot water . . . or cold water, on occasion.

I can remember getting a brand-new pair of shoes presented to me – then promptly losing one them in the river. I'd been warned never to go near the water, but unfortunately I didn't always follow orders. When I was down on the bank kicking stones into the river, one of my brand-new shoes flew off and disappeared downstream. I had to go home with my tail between my legs and tell my parents what had happened, but I knew I couldn't let on where I'd been. Instead, I told them I'd lost the shoe in a burn near the tannery in the town. That still wasn't great, but it was better to admit to having been playing there than at the big river.

The water ran under the sheds where the cattle hides were worked on, and I told my father that my shoe had disappeared into the tunnel, knowing he couldn't go looking for it and that would be the end of it. Or so I thought. He gathered up some friends and went wading into the water and through that dark tunnel, searching for this damn shoe. Of course, I knew they wouldn't find it, but it was too late to say anything. I ended up feeling the instep of his shoe on my backside, something that happened whenever I got out of hand. It was nothing serious but enough to show me who was boss.

In truth, I was never a bad lad and always had a disciplined streak in me. That served me well in later life and I think it endeared me to authority figures, as they knew I could be relied on to toe the line, even though I could be stubborn and would stand up to people I thought were in the wrong.

Standing up to people is one thing; animals were quite another. We used to go down to the river to collect eggs from the ducks, and I remember all too well getting caught in an open field with a raging bull. I had all my eggs in a bag and had to climb a tree to get away from the beast, then throw eggs at it from up on my branch to try to get it to leave me alone. It didn't work. Instead, it stood there even angrier than it had been before but now covered in yolks. It was a long afternoon while I waited for my opportunity to scarper.

It was all part of growing up in Scotland. I'd go down and swim in the river, and I just generally enjoyed having the countryside all around us, although we lived in the middle of the town at that time.

I went to primary school in Cupar, although when we eventually moved on to Perth for my father's venture into the pub trade, it led to a change for me, too, as we were uprooted. In hindsight, it was the best thing that ever happened to me.

I went to Balhousie Boys' School, housed in a grand old red-brick building typical of the time. Of course, the school is now open to boys and girls, and it has grown and been modernised over the years, but driving past the old place still brings the memories flooding back.

Perhaps the fact there were other, more important events going on at home has a part to play in how vivid my recollections of that time are. I was just in my mid-teens when my father died. He was only 39 when he died in 1947.

It was the ulcers he had first suffered from back in Fife that eventually killed him, although his new line of work didn't help. In the pub game, you can get pally with the wrong type of people, and I always thought he didn't look after himself as well as he should have done when he was working in the bar.

I remember the doctor was throwing pills at him all the time, but to no avail. Eventually, his health problems caught up with him and he suddenly fell seriously ill. There was an emergency operation to try to save him, but it was all too late and there was nothing that could be done.

It was a terrible shock for everyone, not least my mother. She had not only lost her husband but had to face up to life as a single parent. She also had to carry on in the pub – not the easiest trade for a woman to be involved in, particularly in the 1940s and '50s, when it was very much a man's world. Mum tried to get me involved in the business, but I was always adamant that it wasn't for me. It just didn't appeal. By then, I was playing for East Fife, and I didn't want to get tied down to the long hours and the commitment that that type of enterprise requires. It's an unforgiving trade at the best of times.

Mum was a strong woman and she made it work on her own at The Palace, the family's pub on George Street in Perth. It isn't open as a bar any more, although you can still make out the building if you look closely. I drove past not so long ago, a wee trip down memory lane.

Eventually, the pub was sold, with the change of ownership going through within weeks of me joining Rangers. I've often wondered if I made the right decision not to take it on when it was offered to me, particularly in light of the direction my life was taking at that stage. If I had been in the place as a Rangers player, it could have been a real goldmine while I was at my peak and for years after I'd finished in the game, with supporters passing through the bar. The Rangers connection can count for a lot and would have been a big plus for me. But, in truth, it was never something I wanted to do in my heart of hearts.

My wife and I did end up in the hospitality trade eventually, but running a country hotel in the Highlands, as we did, was a very different proposition from life in a town-centre pub, and I never really regretted not taking up the offer of carrying on with the bar. I was still young at that point and it would have been a huge responsibility to take on at that stage in my life.

I had other thoughts about the road ahead, although I didn't have a hard and fast plan. When you are playing football, you tend not to look too far into the future. At the back of my mind, though, I always fancied wending my way to the Highlands. That's exactly the way it transpired in the end, and I can be happy with the way it panned out.

If things had worked out differently, I might still be in Perth and in a very different line of work from sport or the pub trade. While I was starting out in football, I had a job in Perth as a dental technician, making false teeth and other items, and spent a good couple of years in that. I think I would have gone on to make a good career in that profession, and it certainly wouldn't have been a hardship for me if I had ended up going in that direction.

What will be will be. I'm a great believer in tackling whatever life throws at you and have had plenty to keep me occupied down through the years.

13

A SPORTING CHANCE

BOXING GLOVES OR FOOTBALL BOOTS: that was the choice I had to make as a boy. It could quite easily have been a career in the ring rather than on the pitch that I found myself involved in if I'd followed in the footsteps of my father.

Strictly speaking, he was an amateur boxer, but he didn't necessarily follow that ethos to the letter. He might not have been a professional in the full meaning of the word, but he still made a good few pounds from the sport.

Dad and his two brothers used to fight in the booths when the travelling shows came to town. Those fairs went from town to town with their big tents and were a huge draw wherever they went. The booths had been going strong for more than a century by that point and were part and parcel of life. There was always a buzz around the fairs, generated by the fights, and many a big-name champion came from that very background.

It wasn't some back-street, bare-knuckle affair. This was properly organised and serious stuff – and big business for the organisers. Crowds would quickly gather for their boxing fix; at the time, live boxing on television was still very much a rarity. The BBC had started the ball rolling in the late 1930s with the first bout on TV, but generally speaking if you wanted to see a fight you had to get out of your armchair and go and watch one in the flesh. The travelling booths catered for that. In every town they visited, they would find willing opponents – some more qualified than others, I imagine – and vocal crowds ready to cheer on their local favourites.

Apparently, I'm not the only footballer to have come from the same sort of bloodstock. I read not so long ago that Bobby and Jack Charlton's dad was a regular on the circuit in their native North-east, winning the pound it cost to buy their mother an engagement ring in one of his fairground bouts.

The booths continued to thrive long after my father's heyday, although, like everything, they fell victim to a more safety-conscious society. When the British Boxing Board of Control started to stamp its authority on the sport, the tradition began to die out, and by the 1970s they had all but disappeared. Mind you, I'm told that if you venture far enough you can still find a boxing booth, if that's your idea of entertainment. Germany, I believe, still does a roaring trade with them.

In my childhood, the fairs were a really well-organised set-up, with the boxing ring a big part of the entertainment. They'd come to Fife regularly enough and it became a good little earner for the family. Dad and my uncles would go and challenge the resident fighters, play them at their own game. My dad wasn't a ruffian by any measure, but he knew how to handle himself and didn't fear anyone – he didn't have to.

By all accounts, he did very nicely for himself in his regular challenge matches, coming up against men who handed out hammerings for a living day in and day out. Some of the booth fighters could get through more than 15 local contenders in a day, as the doors stayed open for paying punters from early morning through to late at night.

I never saw my father box in the booths. I was a young boy and he would never have encouraged me to go along. It was a pretty rough and ready environment, after all, and one better left to the men. However, as I grew older he did do a bit of amateur boxing in the more traditional sense and I saw him perform in the ring then.

He loved it and had a pair of boxing gloves on my hands by the time I was six or seven, down on his hands and knees sparring with me whenever we had a few minutes spare. I had to learn to move well and hold my own, and I never forgot those lessons. I also carried with me the sense that I was equipped to look after myself if need be, wherever I landed up.

I think my father realised that I didn't share his enthusiasm for the Queensberry Rules. In our days in Cupar, he got me an old football to kick around, although that was never really his sport. I showed some promise in the ring, obviously borrowing from my dad's talents, but I preferred to have a ball at my feet than gloves on my hands.

When we moved to Perth, the YMCA in the town had a boxing set-up. During my schooldays, I used to do a bit in the ring when I was down at the club, but nothing more serious than a spot of sparring. I always said I didn't want to get mixed up in the sport at any great level. After all, I had my good looks to protect.

At one stage, I got talked into having a wee bout – and the bugger broke my nose. I was sixteen, and he was four inches taller and three stone heavier than me. He wasn't supposed to go all out, but he did, and I thought then that it wasn't something I wanted to let happen again.

That reinforced my opinion that I wasn't interested in boxing competitively. The only thing I was interested in was making sure that if there were problems, whether for me or my friends and colleagues, I could handle myself and sort them out. I was never a thug, but people knew I would stick up for myself and those on my side. I like to think 'hard but fair' would be a better description.

I would always stand up for what I thought was right. If that meant ruffling a few feathers, and I certainly had to do that many times over the years, then so be it. You can't let people push you around in any walk of life.

With my interest in boxing on the back burner, my true love of football began to flourish after the family's move through to Perth, and I started playing for the YMCA and the school team. I began to get a little bit better, then a little bit better again, eventually going on to play in the juvenile leagues and the juniors.

Those who saw me play in later years, when I was seen very much as a stopper rather than a creator, might be surprised to learn that I made my name in my youth as a goal-scoring centre-forward. The fact that I was big and strong was as useful to me while I was playing up front as it was when I dropped further back.

My efforts on the football pitch were helped in no small part by the athleticism that came naturally to me. After moving up to Balhousie Boys' School, I won the school sports championship by doing well in track sports like the 100 yards and half-mile races, as well as in putting the shot and other field events. I really enjoyed the competition and was getting stronger and faster all the time. I've still got a newspaper clipping from the time of me being lifted shoulder high by my friends, medal round my neck and proud as punch. I loved the spirit of competition, not to mention the bragging rights that went with being sports champion.

In saying that, it wasn't all golds and glory. I'll never forget getting myself in a right fankle with the shot-put, with the PE teacher showing me the textbook way to do it . . . and me coming in a lowly third. I went back to him after the competition had finished, grabbed hold of the shot and lobbed it any old way. It sailed off into the distance, easily a winning throw – too late for me, though.

As well as making a few headlines on the track, I was a county swimmer and could hold my own in the pool at that level. I enjoyed swimming; it was as pure a sport as you could get, and if you didn't do well you had only yourself to blame, no teammates or equipment to deflect attention.

I liked the discipline of training, too, and pushing myself hard. I had a good engine even as a teenager, and I think that stamina came naturally to me. I was able to build on it by working hard, but you need the bedrock to start with. Because I was fit, I pretty much turned my hand to anything sporty. I did well in table tennis, winning a medal or two in that.

But it was when I won the school sports championship that I first became aware that I had something in me – a sporting chance, if you like. Then when I was in juvenile football I got offers to go to senior clubs as far afield as Burnley.

I must have been 15 when I was invited down there to have a spell with them, but I took homesick and didn't go, even though I had my tickets in my hand and everything. I was all set for it, but at the last minute I couldn't get on the train and go.

Jimmy Scott, the father of the *Sunday Post* sportswriter Ronnie, was the Burnley scout in the Dundee area, and he put in a power of work to unearth good young Scottish players to join the cause. They had quickly discovered that there was a decent pool of talent to pick from and that if they were better organised than the local clubs they could nip in before them.

Jimmy hadn't been a player at that level himself, but he obviously had a good eye. He discovered the likes of Bobby Seith, who later returned from England to star in Dundee FC's championship-winning side of the 1960s, and a whole host of other great players. He went on to scout for Preston North End after Burnley's manager Frank Hill had moved to Lancashire.

Hill knew Tayside well himself. He was a Forfar boy who had made good, playing for his home-town team before progressing to Aberdeen and Scotland, then heading south with Arsenal in the 1930s. Under Hill, Burnley had a nucleus of Scots at the club. It was when they showed an interest that it first dawned on me that I might have a future in professional football rather than perhaps in track and field.

I knew I was fit enough for it, and when teams like St Johnstone and Dundee United, not to mention Burnley, started talking about taking me on, it seemed like it was something that could work for me. It was there at the back of my mind, but it wasn't the be-all and end-all for me at that stage in my life. I think I was very much of the opinion that what would be would be. I was content to let things take their natural course and see where that took me.

I was playing my football with Perth City Boys Club and Huntingtower, who were going great guns at that time. There were some cracking players in both the Perth and Huntingtower sides. My performances attracted attention from just about every junior club in Perth and some back in Fife, too. I was still playing in the forward line at that stage. It was in the juniors that I dropped back to play half-back and full-back, so that I could use my power and pace to better effect. The rest, as they say, is history.

Eventually, I plumped for Newburgh, taking me back to my roots in Fife, after scoring a couple of goals during a trial match against Auchterarder Primrose, and signed on the dotted line in the summer of 1950, not realising what I was letting myself in for. Although I wasn't yet aware of it, the grade had a reputation for being rough and ready – it still does – and it turned out to be that way in my experience.

Turning junior was quite a big step when I was still young enough to be playing juvenile football. In my first game, I was playing centre-forward against a brute of a centre-half, a 6-ft 2-in. hairy-arsed character who clearly didn't think much of the young upstart he was facing. There had been a bit of publicity when I'd been signed, so clearly he had my number. Without warning, with the ball away at the opposite end of the field, he came up and kneed me in the back so hard that I went down in a crumpled heap. My kidneys felt as though they were about to explode. It was agony. He walked away and not another soul saw it.

As I dropped to the floor, I thought about calling it quits then and there, but I got back on my feet and hobbled about for a while, catching my breath. I could either give up there and then or throw myself back into the thick of the action and try to hold my own. I went for the latter and never looked back.

At Newburgh, I had a reputation for being quite fast, and when the Highland games season came around the rest of the boys decided I should enter the race at the local games and they would put some money on me to win. I arrived early in the village and decided to stop for a cup of coffee at a wee café just up the road from the pitch. I ordered my coffee and then the smell of warm pies started wafting out of the kitchen. I was feeling a bit peckish, so I tucked into a couple of them for an early lunch while I was at it. It turned out that wasn't advisable when you were about to run a 400-yard race, and not surprisingly I lost. In fact, I struggled to make it round the track at all! I'd discovered why they fed horses before a race if they wanted them to lose it. The boys were all wondering what had happened, but I didn't dare to tell them. Lesson learned.

That was just a minor glitch during my time with the club. My performances were steady and consistent, with senior clubs still keeping a close eye on my progress. Dundee and St Mirren were said to be keen, but it was Everton and East Fife who came forward with offers in the final shake-up.

A certain Scot Symon was manager at Bayview at the time, and Mr Symon's powers of persuasion proved strong enough to keep me in Fife. He had been a playing legend with Rangers and was a big name for East Fife to land when they appointed him as manager in 1947. He went on to spend six seasons with the club and proved to be an inspired appointment, taking his team up to the First Division and winning the League Cup twice in his six years in charge. In the year I joined, 1950, the attendance record was broken when more than 22,500 crammed into the old ground for a derby against Dunfermline, so he didn't have to give me the hard sell to convince me it was a good club to be joining.

There was a tremendous amount of respect for the man – not surprisingly, given his achievements – and he clearly knew exactly what he was building. He took East Fife as high as third in the league before being tempted south by Preston, who were one of the big guns at that time.

I had only a small part to play in what he achieved at East Fife, but I was always glad of the opportunity he afforded me as a youngster starting out in the game. I'm a great believer that you have to be lucky and have to be in the right place at the right time for the right people to see you – but you also have to work hard. There were plenty of boys who could have played senior level but didn't, and that was down to details: namely, heart and determination, the two things you can't coach.

Those were the qualities that got me my break with East Fife, those were the qualities that got me through the dark days in Korea and Japan, and those were the qualities that were to get me a shot at the big time with Rangers. Life was about to change forever.

14

BECOMING PART OF THE FAMILY

A SINGLE BUTTON, BUT ONE that could strike fear and trepidation into the heart of a grown man. I'd pulled triggers on machine guns and pins of grenades . . . but that switch outside the manager's office at Ibrox was far more daunting than either of those.

To put you in the picture, when you were called upstairs you would press the button outside and one of two lights would come on: 'Enter' or 'Wait'. Not 'Please Wait', just 'Wait'. It was never 'Enter'. You always had to sit outside, alone with your thoughts, wondering why you'd been hauled up in the first place, more often than not. It was a bit like being sent to the headmaster's office.

I can remember sitting outside, waiting for that all-important light to go on, just after I'd signed for the club. My first experience of the manager's office. I sat there with my young life flashing through my mind – everything I'd gone through in Korea, it was all being replayed. I suppose that was the first time I'd actually sat down and thought about where I'd been and where I'd arrived at. To make it to Ibrox, up that marble staircase, was the stuff of dreams. Thinking about the nightmare I'd been through in the war, it began to sink in how big a break I had been given. At the same time, I knew that you had to make your own luck; sitting there outside the office was just the beginning: I had to grab that opportunity and run with it. I'd never been more determined in my life.

Having gone via the juniors in Perthshire to Bayview in Fife and then on to Korea, I hadn't taken a straightforward route to Ibrox. Before I joined Rangers, I had played only a handful of games for East Fife: three, to be precise. The war had taken me out of the equation, although I was still signed to East Fife when I returned to Scotland for my rehabilitation. But it soon became clear my future was not in Methil; it was to be west rather than east that I would be heading.

As I mentioned, Davie Kinnear had seen me come through the various stages of my recovery. Having arrived at Bridge of Earn Hospital barely able to do any more than walk, I'd built my strength and stamina to a level that impressed even him – and Davie was a hard taskmaster. It was his nod to Scot Symon at Rangers that set the wheels in motion. With the pair of them convinced I'd done enough to prove my fitness, I was whisked off to Ibrox by the manager.

I was still on the East Fife books, though, so money had to change hands. Scot Symon paid the princely sum of £1,250 to sign me in 1956, presumably being able to use his links to Bayview to smooth the deal. In fact, 'the Boss', as I always called him, was accused by the press of 'stealing' me from East Fife. In reply, he simply pointed out that they had agreed to the transfer and that I hadn't even been a regular in the first team at Methil in any case. There was a bit of truth in that, although he hadn't given them much time to use me before he nipped in with the offer. It was the second time he'd signed me, so he must have seen something in me that he thought would be useful to his team.

There were no agents and no protracted negotiations. From the minute I heard that Rangers were interested in signing me, my mind was made up. I was at a crossroads in my life in any case, looking towards life after the Army and deciding what path to follow. Obviously, a full-time job in football was a dream for me, but I certainly wasn't banking on it. When it became clear that it was an option, it was like all of my Christmases had come early. I simply couldn't wait to get started.

As I say, there was no question of negotiation when it came to contracts. You took what you were given and trusted that the club and the manager would look after you, which they did, up to a point. We certainly didn't live like kings, let's put it like that, but it was a comfortable life.

Vi and I were due to be married soon after I signed, so it was the start of a new life for both of us. Up to that point, we had been living in Perth and considering what the future held and whether I should follow my mum into the family pub. Instead, it transpired that my new job would take us to Glasgow, the city that would become our home for more than a decade and a half. I'd travelled through to Ibrox when I'd first got word that Rangers were interested in signing me, and everything had been signed and sealed.

By way of a welcome, the Boss and the club helped to find Vi and me a flat to set up home in. It was on Harrison Drive, just off the Copland Road and over the back from the ground, which was a handy five-minute walk from the front door for me each morning. It meant I really did eat, sleep and breathe Rangers, since the club was just a corner kick away. We had many happy times there, with great neighbours and a real sense of community spirit, and we lived in the same spot for fully eight years, so there are plenty of good memories from that part of the city. We quickly fell in love with Glasgow life.

I should point out that when I say the club helped us find the flat, I mean just that. They helped find it, but they certainly didn't pay for it like you hear about with players relocating today. No, the rent came from my fairly modest pay packet and there was never any question of favours being done.

In fact, when it was time to leave the club in 1964, I got an unexpected letter from Mr Symon, c/o Rangers Football Club. It wasn't a bonus to thank me for my service, nor was it a note to pass on his appreciation of my efforts. No, it was a bill for £17 to cover the remainder of the lease on the flat we were leaving behind. I've still got that letter tucked away, among the other keepsakes from the time. There were no flies on him, that's for sure – and no danger of the club getting itself into any financial bother with that type of approach to managing the money. It just shows you that the idea that footballers led a charmed life back then isn't accurate; we had to pay our way and earn our keep like everyone else. We were heading to a new house on the other side of the city at that point, so we settled up and waved farewell to 'our' place on Harrison Drive.

Eight years previously, we were all excited about moving there in the first place, about the bright lights and the new challenges in every aspect of our life after I'd signed the contract to move to Ibrox. It was as the ink dried that it began to dawn on me what I was about to embark upon. As a country boy, I was in awe of the whole set-up. I'd never even been to Glasgow before that first visit to Ibrox, so going to work there, at Rangers Football Club of all places, was an incredible step for me.

Walking through the door for the first time, reporting for duty, was a nerve-racking affair. I was confident in my ability, confident in my fitness. But until I got my first few sessions under my belt, there was always going to be a bit of trepidation. I'm the first to admit I was in awe of the legends I found myself working alongside. Players like Sammy Baird, Johnny Hubbard, Billy Simpson and Ian McColl were all massive characters in the dressing-room and fantastic players into the bargain. I had tremendous respect for the men I could now call colleagues, but I realised I had to prove myself able to live in that type of company.

The main man I had to win over wasn't the manager or anyone

else on the backroom staff, it was George Young, captain of club and country and a legend of the Scottish game. By then, he was reaching the twilight of his career and was carrying a bit more weight than he had done at his peak, but he was still a formidable player and a very influential character both on and off the park.

The problem was, I think, that George feared I was there to take the shirt off his back. He knew he was coming towards the end of the road and he viewed me as his successor, brought in under his nose. Our early relationship was cagey, to say the least, but in time we became great friends. I understood how he felt; he had visions I would be the one who would eventually push him out the door, and that is not a nice feeling for anyone. When he eventually left the club, it was then that our friendship blossomed and we discovered we got on very well together.

I counted myself fortunate to have been able to work alongside George, even if it was at the end of his days in the game, while I was also lucky to work with others who were at the start of their careers. People like John Greig and Willie Henderson came through the ranks while I was at Ibrox, and I tried to do my bit to help them along the way. In many ways, I was one of those who bridged that gap between the old guard and the new, along with people like Eric Caldow, Bobby Shearer and Alex Scott: more great names and an indication of the quality that we had at the club at that time.

It's fair to say that George was part of clique of older players when I first arrived, understandably so, I suppose, since they had been there, done it and seen it all. He, along with George Niven, Eric Caldow and Sammy Baird, ruled the roost, and I found quite quickly that Sammy considered himself to be top dog. I would say I got on fine with everyone pretty much from day one, everyone apart from Mr Baird. The two of us never saw eye to eye, and while we never resorted to throwing punches, there wasn't much love lost.

He wanted to be the main man and I wanted to take him down a peg or two, especially when I saw the way he treated some of the kids on the ground staff. He'd order them to clean his boots, to do this and do that. I didn't think he was going about it the right way and wasn't afraid to tell him about it. Looking back, I was probably a bit bold, but such is life.

When I was recruited in 1956, I was joining a club that looked to be going places. They had just won the First Division championship, the fifth time the title flag had been flying over Ibrox since normal service had been resumed after the Second World War. Aberdeen, Celtic and Hibs (three times) had also picked up the league trophy in those post-war years, but Rangers were very much the team in the ascendancy, and under Scot Symon they were building for the future. The Boss had taken over from Bill Struth just a couple of years before I arrived, and he was slowly and surely putting his own mark on the squad and on the club.

He was a tough man, a strict man. Having come from army life, that wasn't something that fazed me, and I responded well to the discipline and the work ethic in which Mr Symon believed. He had been schooled in the ways of Rangers by Bill Struth, having by all accounts been an utterly dependable player at Ibrox before and after the war. Having played for the club and for Scotland, he spoke from a position of authority, and there was never any doubt that he had the respect of the dressing-room.

His achievements as a manager also stood up to examination, not least what he had done with East Fife when he'd first started out. I'd seen that at close quarters, of course, and I could understand exactly why Rangers, from the outside looking in, had moved to appoint him themselves. After moving to Bayview in 1947, he'd spent six seasons there, winning the League Cup twice, not to mention taking the club to the top three in the big league. Will East Fife ever see the likes again? I doubt it.

He arrived at Rangers via a short stop at Preston North End and was really still settling in when he signed me. It was a team in transition in many ways, with many loyal Struth players nearing the natural end of their careers and voids to be filled. It would take a big man to take on that job and, in Symon, the Rangers board chose very wisely indeed. Just like his predecessor, he would go to extraordinary lengths to try to gain an advantage for Rangers. The attention to detail was incredible and his reach knew no bounds.

For example, the football boot 'favoured' at Rangers – with a little bit of persuasion from Mr J.S. Symon – was designed by a certain Scot Symon. The manager clearly had his own ideas about what a boot should look and feel like, and I suppose you would have to credit him for his attention to detail. There couldn't be too many coaches who went to those lengths, with these 'Symon Specials' manufactured in bulk for all the boys to wear.

One day, the manager of the Co-operative boot and shoe factory in Glasgow contacted me and asked if I'd go and see him at their offices on Paisley Road. I did just that, and it turned out that they had a new design of football boot that he wanted to run past me. A week later, I turned up at his office and he presented me with a shiny new pair of the latest model, fresh off the production line and made from a lovely soft leather that would give far better touch and control. I tried them on and they fitted like a glove. They were a little different to Mr Symon's tackety boots, that was for sure, and closer to today's football boots – or slippers, as I like to think of them!

The first training session I pitched up to in my special footwear was something to behold. I was all stripped and ready for action, with my brand spanking new boots neatly laced and ready to go, when the manager came into the dressing-room. It took about two seconds for him to clock them – and I won't repeat what he had to say to me. The abridged version would be: 'Those are not for you, Harold, not for you.' So it was out with the new, in with the old tackety affairs.

That little incident was a good while into my Rangers career. In the early days, I was keeping my head down. It took me a bit of time to feel like I belonged in the company of the more established players, I suppose.

I was eased into Rangers life as a reserve player, and one of my first outings was against the Celtic second string. Charlie Tully, a legend at Parkhead but winding down at that stage, was the man I was up against. In truth, he should have been enjoying his retirement by that point, but they'd given him an extra season in the reserves to play his way out gently. To me, he wasn't over-the-hill Charlie Tully, he was superstar Charlie Tully. So when he picked up the ball early in the game, I produced a Harold Davis special and near enough put him into the front row of the stand. The next time he got the ball, I did exactly the same. The next time . . . you can guess the rest. Eventually, he turned to me and said, 'Look, son, if you just lay off me I'll give you the bloody ball!'

After a somewhat over-enthusiastic start to my career, I soon found my stride, and it wasn't long before I pushed my way to the fringes of the first team and got my chance to make a mark.

Within a couple of months of being a Rangers player, I had pressmen suggesting I was already pushing for international honours. It was flattering, but I tried not to have my head turned by that sort of thing. Headlines didn't tend to sway managers, and it was the Boss at Rangers I was most interested in impressing. I'd got my chance; now I had to take it.

15

A NICE START TO IBROX LIFE

IF MY INTRODUCTION TO RESERVE football had been notable thanks to my tussle with Charlie Tully, the start I had in the first team was pretty remarkable too. One of the first games I ever played was in the European Cup against the French champions, Nice. Talk about in at the deep end!

It was the 1956–57 season and the very first time the club had been involved in European competition, so everything was new to us. In a way, it made it easier for a rookie like me to be involved, because even the most experienced campaigners were having to learn the ropes as far as the Continental game was concerned.

So was everyone else, though, given that the European Cup had come into existence only the year before. The French had been the driving force behind the competition – and obviously thought they stood a good chance of doing well. They hadn't bargained on their neighbours across the border in Spain, though. Real Madrid won the trophy for the first five years, so they clearly had the measure of the opposition from all corners.

For us, in that first-ever European tie, it was the French opposition we had to concern ourselves with. Nice had won their league, just pipping Lille to the title. We had won ours, beating Aberdeen to the punch. So it was Scotland v. France and we were all set for it.

I wasn't part of the team for the first two games but a very interested spectator. Our first-ever European tie was played at Ibrox in the October of 1956, when Nice came calling. We'd gone into the competition at the second-round stage, and we knew they would be a class act.

That certainly proved to be the case and, watching that game, it became clear that the old Scottish up-and-at-them spirit wouldn't be enough at that level of competition. They could move the ball at pace and were comfortable on it, right the way through their side. We had to be at the top of our game and start to think in a slightly different way to cope with the attacking edge they had, but we did it, coming out 2–1 winners in Glasgow. Max Murray and Billy Simpson scored the goals, making their own little bit of history in the process.

The second leg was over in the south of France. Everyone knew what was required, but there was still an acceptance that Nice, especially on their own patch, would be a dangerous proposition. Sure enough, they gave a spirited account of themselves and, despite a Johnny Hubbard goal from the penalty spot, went on to win the match 2–1 and peg it back to 3–3 on aggregate. The away-goal rule wasn't even a twinkle in the eye of the UEFA president at that point, nor was there the horrible prospect of a coin toss to decide who would go out.

Instead, it was ruled that there would be a third leg, a decider. In their wisdom, the powers that be decided that the Parc des Princes, that hulk of a stadium in Paris, would be the best 'neutral' venue for the winner-takes-all tie.

When the final whistle blew to signal the end of the second leg in Nice, I was still a reserve player at Rangers. That was on 14 November, two weeks before the third and final match in Paris and ten days before I made my first-team debut, so it turned out I would have a part to play, despite my complete inexperience of football at any great level. Mind you, I was only expected to be a spectator, there as a squad man rather than to take a place in the team.

However, I was old enough and the manager clearly thought I was good enough, so I had to dig out my passport and pack my suitcase to prepare for our little assignment over the Channel. It was another overseas adventure, but an altogether more pleasant one than my last outing, to Korea. We travelled out hoping we could get the better of them, but playing the match in France did give them an advantage.

On the morning of the game we had breakfast as usual at the team hotel and then went out for a bit of an early warm-up, just to get the legs going and blow the cobwebs away after our trip. There had been some doubts about George Young before we travelled, as he had missed the last league game – a match in which I had deputised for him, making my debut – but he was confident he'd be fine to play. Then, in that little session, he pulled up as we did laps of the pitch. That was it, his chance was gone. There and then, I was told George was out, I was in. What a wake-up call that was on the morning of one of the biggest games the club had ever been involved in!

Very early in the game, it became clear we were in for a torrid evening. The French side came at us with wave after wave of attacks, and I have to say I enjoyed every minute of it. I far preferred being in the thick of the action to being to all intents and purposes a spectator in a one-sided match, with all the play at the other end. This certainly wasn't one of those occasions.

I stood up to the examination pretty well, but the ball kept coming back at us. We just couldn't hold possession. In saying that, I remember Sammy Baird had an absolute stormer up front, so it wasn't one-way traffic.

Nice went ahead just before half-time, but we were back level not long after the break thanks to an own goal. Unfortunately, they grabbed another at the right end as the game drew to a close and, with just 15 minutes to play and as we opened up a bit looking for an equaliser, they made it 3–1 and killed it stone dead when Bobby Shearer was short with a pass back.

On paper, it looked like we'd been given a bit of a going over, but in reality it was another close-run affair. For a chunk of the game, we'd matched them well, but in the final third it was a struggle to create anything that would cut them open. It was my first lesson in Europe, and I have to say I came away a far wiser player even after just 90 minutes in that type of environment. It would stand me in good stead for the years ahead, with many more Continental competitions to face up to and many thousands of miles to rack up along that particular path. I enjoyed tremendous European nights, but that first one against Nice will always stick in my mind.

It was only my second outing with the Rangers first team. It's incredible to think now that I was parachuted in for such a big match when I was so wet behind the ears. My first game had been in the far more familiar but equally daunting surroundings of Ibrox. Running out there to play my first 'proper' game in front of the home crowd was an experience to make the hairs on the back of my neck stand on end. It was a huge thrill for me, the moment I'd been dreaming of since I first got the call from Scot Symon to move to Glasgow.

The match he drafted me in for was a First Division fixture against Aberdeen. It was deep in winter, but I don't remember feeling the cold. I was powered by adrenalin that day and nothing could have knocked me off my stride. As I mentioned, I'd been taken into the team to fill in for the injured George Young, playing centre-half and pulling on 'his' number 5 jersey to play the Dons. We were gunning for the title by that point, having lost only a couple of games in the first part of the season, and a win was vital to keep our championship hopes alive. It all went to plan, thankfully, with a 3–1 victory getting my Rangers career off to a winning start.

Billy Simpson, Max Murray and Johnny Hubbard, with another of his trademark penalties, did the damage.

For me, the main concern was what was happening at the other end of the park and, in particular, with Paddy Buckley. He was my direct opponent on my debut and I couldn't have asked for a sterner test. When Aberdeen had won the league in 1954–55 Buckley had been at the heart of it. He'd scored seventeen goals that season and was one of the stars of the Scottish game in that era; certainly he was Aberdeen's poster boy and a Scotland international to boot.

There was me going head to head with him and wondering what I was letting myself in for, with my opposite number renowned for his pace as much as for his deadly accuracy in front of goal. It was sink-or-swim time for me, and fortunately I remained very much on the surface. It was a tough afternoon, but I managed to keep Buckley quiet in what turned out to be one of the few times I'd face him. He suffered a bad knee injury the next year and had to quit the game – a big loss for Aberdeen.

I'd passed my test with flying colours, but there wasn't any time to reflect on the events of that weekend, as just four days later we were off on our travels to France. Clearly, the defeat in Paris knocked the stuffing out of us a little, but there was enough in the performance to ensure spirits hadn't dipped by the time we returned to domestic action.

I kept my place in the side for the home match against East Fife a few days later, a chance to face my old teammates. There was no room for sentiment, mind you. We blitzed them 6–1, and I have to say I enjoyed myself that day. To be part of a well-oiled machine like that was great, perfect for building the confidence of a man new to the scene. I'd played three games in the space of a week, so by the end of it I was already feeling like a fully fledged first-teamer.

I dipped back out when George returned from his injury, but I

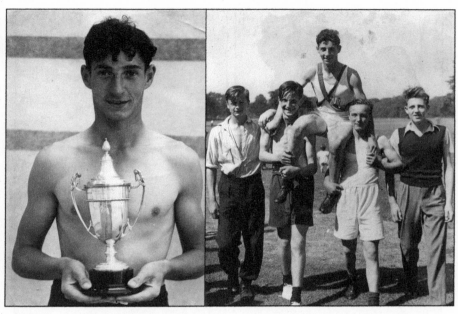

Early success: this trophy came not from football but from my dalliance with swimming as a promising schoolboy competitor.

On a high: that's me being held aloft after sports success during my schooldays in Perth.

Team spirit: this is the Newburgh juniors team of the late 1940s. That's me on the far left in the front row.

Family life: Vi with my mother early in our life together.

Kitted out: resplendent in army uniform before heading off for active service.

On the ocean wave: I have vivid memories of my time on the HMS *Empire Pride* during its service as a troop-ship.

Home comforts: the camps in Korea became a second home to the British troops and our allies.

No rest: taking care of domestic duties during a break from fighting.

Good company: that's me with fellow C Company soldiers in Korea.

Battleground: part of the dreaded Hook, which saw fierce fighting.

Danger zone: still smiling while out on the line.

Ready for action: kitted out in my army football gear for the tournament in Korea.

Away tie: the pitch cleared on the edge of the war zone to provide some light relief.

Behind the Iron Curtain: this was one of the illicit snaps taken with the camera I smuggled onto our Russian tour. I'm pictured in Moscow with the young John Greig (left) and Ralph Brand (centre).

Boy in blue: I finally made it to Ibrox after a long battle back to fitness. That's me second from right in the back row in the 1960–61 team photo.
(Courtesy of Eric McCowat Archives)

Glory days: I'm pictured here (second from right) celebrating another trophy success during my time at Rangers. This was after the 1962 Scottish Cup final win against St Mirren. (Courtesy of Eric McCowat Archives)

Sporting passion: golf was a big part of the
social scene at Rangers.

Happy couple: Vi has been by my
side through the highs and lows of
life as a soldier, sportsman, hotelier
and in our retirement.

Lucky escape: this is what was left of our car after
our road accident in the Highlands.

Bionic man: the metal frame that
was used to get me back on my
feet after the car accident.

Country life: fishing is my big
passion now, with Vi and I settled in
the Highlands, close to some of the
best lochs and rivers in the world.

didn't have to wait long for another chance, with Willie Logie the next man I filled in for, in a home match against Hearts just a couple of weeks later. I was moved to left-half, slotting into Willie's place against the Edinburgh side in the league in December 1956. It was that game that saw me really establish myself, and I remember it well.

The rain was hammering down for the entire 90 minutes and the pitch was absolutely sodden. It didn't bother me one bit and I strolled through an eventful first half, with Hearts 2–1 up and looking to hold that lead going into the break. Then, just a couple of minutes before the interval, I popped up with the equaliser. It was a fantastic feeling to get that first goal for Rangers, made all the better by the fact it was a belter. Ian McColl had pushed his way forward and squared the ball to Billy Simpson, but he heard my call and let the ball run into my path in time for me to thunder a shot past the keeper from all of 25 yards.

It didn't get any quieter when we came out for the second half; I was crocked in a challenge with Dave Mackay just after the restart. I tried to keep going but ended up making it worse and had to limp off the park. After ten minutes or so of frantic treatment, I was able to go back on and at least make up the numbers by playing outside-left. As it happened, I started coming into my own out on the wing and had a whale of a time. We went on to win 5–3, staying on course for the league title.

After my exploits in keeping Paddy Buckley under the cosh when we'd played Aberdeen a few weeks earlier, I'd now gone up against Mackay – the hard man of the Hearts set-up and another giant of the Scottish game. I'd given as good as I got, and the consensus afterwards was that I'd come off the best in that one. It gave me the confidence to go up against anyone and everyone from then on in. I'd faced the best and hadn't found anything to be scared of, so any nervousness that I might have had quickly evaporated. From a personal point of view, I really began to feel accepted that day, not just by my teammates but also by the supporters and the media. I earned my stripes, if you like.

Although Willie Logie came back in for a few games, I ended up making the number 6 jersey my own in the second half of the season and went on to play more than half the league fixtures as we galloped on to win the league. It was the first of many trophies I would win with Rangers, a piece of the club's history that I was able to play a part in.

It was a period of time during which interest in our achievements was soaring, buoyed by the success we enjoyed. Crowds were huge at that time. Anything less than 40,000 was a disappointment and it wasn't unusual to have between 60,000 and 80,000 in the ground. Cup finals were at least 100,000 every time.

Winning cups and competitions became a habit at Rangers, but medals were not the be-all and end-all for me. In 2009, I was inducted into the Rangers Hall of Fame. It was a huge honour for me, and the kind words expressed at the time meant a lot. When I look at the list of wonderful Rangers men on the list, I feel humbled to be among them. Like so many others, I always gave my all when I pulled on that jersey, and to have been part of such a wonderful team – and a fantastic club – was the most incredible experience.

16

A EUROPEAN MISSION

THERE'S ALWAYS ONE THAT GETS away. For me, that one was a European winner's medal. We came close, just a whisker – one game – away from getting that prize on the shelf.

Ibrox always had a great atmosphere, but that was especially true on the big European nights. It was inspiring for the home players, intimidating for the visitors. With that behind us, we had a wonderful platform to go on and do well in the Continental competitions, and we certainly did that, with some more than decent performances.

In the 1960–61 season, we went all the way to the final of the European Cup-Winners' Cup, proving that Scottish teams could live with the best in the world when it came to club football. I was fortunate to play against just about every nation you could think of during that period: the French, the Spanish, English teams and everything in between. Our final paired us with the Italians of Fiorentina – a real test if ever there was one. They had been runners-up in Serie A the previous season, second only to the impressive Juventus team of that era, and that told us something about what we could expect when we faced them.

It was the only time the European Cup-Winners' Cup final was played over two legs, and I don't think it was necessarily to our advantage. When you play a one-off cup final, it is cut and dried: you are going out there to win, no grey area. Over two legs, there's a different mentality and so many issues to cloud it. Do you attack at home with your crowd behind you? Do you keep it tight in the first leg and go all out in the second? What's a comfortable lead to take into the second tie? One goal? Two goals? All of those questions and more have to be taken into consideration, and it almost becomes more of a game of chess than a football match.

As it happened, we were at home in the first leg, and Fiorentina would have to sample that Ibrox atmosphere. The Italians were past masters at playing cutely; we knew they would come to Ibrox looking to shut us out and take us back to Florence to try to finish the job.

They ended up leaving Glasgow with more than they could have hoped for: a 2–0 win. I was held accountable for the opening goal, with a back pass to Billy Ritchie being intercepted by one of the Italian forwards. It will go down in history as my mistake, but I still reckon if Billy had come off his line he would have got to it first. Not that I'd criticise Billy too much; he was a great servant to the club.

They'd opened the scoring just twelve minutes into the match, and they grabbed another one in the final minute to give the type of cushion they could only have dreamt of before they touched down in Scotland.

Our cause wasn't helped by the fact that the Scotland contingent in our squad had also just flown into the country, having been away on international duty in Czechoslovakia a couple of days previously. Not that any of them would use it as an excuse. We were all professionals, paid to play the game, and would never complain about the number of matches we faced. If we could have played every day of the week, we would gladly have done so, and we were all itching to get out on the park against Fiorentina.

It was a lively atmosphere, to say the least, on and off the park. The police were kept on their toes as passion in the crowd threatened to boil over. At one stage, officers dragged a fan the full width of the pitch during a break in the play. It looked a bit on the heavy-handed side, I'd have to say.

The Italians set the tone of the evening with some meaty challenges. Naturally, we matched them on that score. They weren't going to come to our place and intimidate us. It wasn't the physical side of the game that let us down; it was simply an inability to put the ball in the back of the net.

We had chances – including a penalty that Eric Caldow put wide of the post, with the help of some pretty unsporting Italian tactics – but didn't take them. That miss from the spot wasn't typical of Eric, and the grumble at the time was that the visiting keeper, Enrico Albertosi, had moved when he was taking his run-up. Either way, we lost the tie and had an uphill battle when we flew over to Italy for the next game.

We were going out to Tuscany looking to redress a two-goal deficit, and that was always going to be a tall order. So it proved to be, with a 2–1 defeat out there sealing the result in favour of Fiorentina.

We knew it was a major achievement to reach that final, but the pain of losing it stopped us dwelling on that side of things. It's only now, looking back, that I can appreciate how few Rangers players have had the privilege of representing the club on that stage.

The surviving members of the class of '61 had a walk-on part in 2008 when Walter Smith's team took on Fiorentina in their UEFA Cup final, which was a nice gesture by the club, and we were well received by the crowd. There we were, more than forty years on, and up to that point only two other Rangers teams had managed to make it through to a European final. That 2008 team was about to become the fourth, but it still shows how few and far between those appearances have been.

The fact that we had come close in 1961 to winning a European competition probably gave us the impression that we would be there or thereabouts every single year we played in Europe. Apart from that, in the 1959–60 season we'd almost reached the final of the European Cup. We'd played Eintracht Frankfurt in the semi-final, however, and they had taught us a bit of a lesson. It ended 12–4 on aggregate, so it's fair to say the best team won. We could have laid down and cowered in a corner, but we didn't. We went away, regrouped and came back an awful lot stronger for the experience, going on that wonderful run to the final the following year.

The European Cup-Winners' Cup was a whole new competition, introduced for that 1960–61 season, and there was a buzz surrounding it. We played Ferencváros in the first round and won the first leg 4–2 at Ibrox. It should have been comfortable, but we didn't like to do things the easy way, and when we fell 2–0 down in the return tie in Hungary we started to get a few nerves fluttering. Davie Wilson came to the rescue, scoring after an hour or so to make it 5–4 on aggregate and carry us through to the quarter-finals. We'd played that game in the national stadium rather than their home ground, simply so they could shoehorn more supporters in.

Next on the agenda were Borussia Mönchengladbach, and again we were on neutral territory, or at least not on their home patch. The game was shifted to Düsseldorf because their stadium wasn't up to scratch, so it took a little bit of the home advantage away from them. I don't think that was the deciding factor, though; we wiped the floor with them, and would have done wherever we'd played them. It ended 3–0 over in Germany and then we trounced them 8–0 back in Glasgow. Ralphie Brand grabbed a hat-trick that night, and we restored a bit of pride after the Eintracht results the previous season.

The semi-final paired us with the mighty Wolverhampton Wanderers – and they were mighty back then. Wolves had been no strangers to the league title in the 1950s and were still going strong into the '60s. The English thought they were superior in any case, something that wasn't helped by the fact their national team had beaten ours 9–3 at Wembley in an international that was played around the time of our ties against Wolves. As it happened, we did our bit for Scottish pride when we beat them 2–0 at Ibrox and went down the road to hold out for a 1–1 draw and go through to the final. I suffered an injury in the first leg and, in the absence of substitutes, ended up being put out on the right wing to see out the game in an area where I couldn't do any damage. As it happened, I ended up getting a second wind and had a bit of a stormer out on the flank. Even the Wolves manager remarked on it after the game, so I must have done something right.

By the end of that campaign, I could consider myself something of a European expert, but at the start of it I was still finding my feet. Mind you, you had to learn quickly because the game at the top level moved fast.

Obviously I'd had that early taste when I was just feeling my way into the team and was pitched in against Nice in the European Cup. I played another tie in the same competition the following season, 1957–58, when we beat Saint-Étienne 3–1 at Ibrox. But it was the year after that I really settled into my stride against the Continentals.

That campaign we were back in the European Cup, the year we ran to the semi-finals and played those ties against Eintracht Frankfurt. The 12–4 defeat against the Germans over two legs was hardly sparkling, but the games we played to get there were impressive. It started with a 7–2 aggregate win against Anderlecht of Belgium in the first round, with a 5–2 win at home setting the tone. After that there was a 5–4 aggregate win against Red Star Bratislava. We beat them 4–3 at home and drew 1–1 over there to go through.

In the quarter-final, we faced Sparta Rotterdam and it took three games to separate us. Unusually, it was the home game that let us down. We went out to the Netherlands for the first leg and beat them 3–2 in a real cracker of a match. We knew the Dutch liked to play football and that gave us space and time to do the same, proving what a good side we were. When they came back to our place, it was a frustrating night; we couldn't get the ball in the net and they nicked one to make it 3–3 on aggregate.

That meant a decider on neutral territory and they picked a wonderful venue for it: Highbury Stadium, the stamping-ground of the mighty Arsenal. We were made to feel at home in London and it inspired us to go on and finish the job. Sammy Baird, with a double, and Jimmy Millar got the goals that gave us a 3–2 win and set up the semi-final.

I'd played in every tie of the competition up to that point and was really revelling in it. Confidence was growing, not just my own but throughout the team. We had a rude awakening against the Germans, however. I was out injured for the first game, over there, which we lost 6–1, and I suppose the damage was done then. But I did play in the 6–3 defeat at home, so I certainly felt some of the pain – not least because we had 70,000 people in the ground for that one. The supporters really took the European competition to their hearts and the crowds were superb. We'd had enormous numbers in for every home game.

After the Cup-Winners' Cup final against Fiorentina, I had another two seasons left in me at European level. In the 1961–62 season, we were back in the European Cup and our decent form continued. We reached the quarter-finals after beating Monaco 6–4 over two legs and then Vorwärts Berlin 6–2 on aggregate. We eventually went out 4–3 to Standard Liège. Losing 4–1 in Belgium in the first game didn't help.

After that, we were back into the European Cup-Winners'

Cup – without quite the same success as we'd had in reaching the '61 final. Not that it wasn't eventful, though!

In the first round, we faced Spanish opposition – Seville – for the first time in the club's history. It was all new to us, but we soon had the measure of them, Jimmy Millar banging in a hat-trick and Ralphie Brand getting his name on the score sheet too, to give us a nice 4–0 cushion before we went over there.

We should have been free and easy in Seville for the second leg, but we walked straight into an ambush. Perhaps we should have predicted it, since they were already getting nasty at Ibrox as things unravelled for them. One or two were making throat-slitting gestures and the like, but to be honest we'd forgotten all about it – until we realised, over in Spain, that maybe they weren't joking!

It was one of those games when my pugilistic talents came in handy, let's put it like that. Nothing could have prepared us for the welcome we received out on that pitch. They absolutely brutalised us; there's no other way to describe it. That was the most vicious and one-sided game I ever played in, and we couldn't do a thing about it.

Most of the stadium was, naturally, filled with Seville supporters, who were very hostile. You could feel the venom coming from the stands. The fans scented blood and their team responded by going out and getting it for them.

It was like another game we'd experienced in Bratislava in a previous season, just a lot worse. We were subjected to horrendous kicking and all-out assaults, with a referee who wasn't taking a blind bit of notice. He was from Portugal and you got the impression there was a bit of neighbourly love going on – either that or he took the approach that he'd do anything for a quiet life. In fact, in the inquest after the game the referee excused us of any blame and admitted he'd let the Spaniards away with murder . . . well, not quite murder – but not far off.

It was the one game where I felt like I had to take control. Bobby Shearer was a tough guy in his own right, and a wonderful Rangers captain, but he wasn't a brutal type of character. I wouldn't say I was either, ordinarily, but this was an exceptional set of circumstances.

It was a bit upside down, because I was telling everyone around me not to retaliate through most of the match – even when the studs were being dragged down our legs and elbows were flailing in our faces. Every dirty trick in the book was being aimed in our direction, but by and large we kept our calm. Then, with about four minutes to go, I'd seen and taken enough of the thuggery that we had absorbed for 86 minutes of the match without any reaction. A straightforward right hook to the chin of the nearest player in a Seville jersey started the recovery of our pride. From that point on, it descended into a real battle, with fists flying left right and centre, but it was one we won. It was as near to a riot as I've ever been involved in, but, after the beating we'd been taking, we felt more than justified in taking the law into our own hands. Nobody else in that stadium was going to protect us, so we went to war.

Even big Doug Baillie, who was a substitute, came wading in to lend his not inconsiderable hands to the cause. It wasn't the bigger fellows like me and Doug who had to watch out, though. The Spaniards seemed to prefer to pick on the little ones, the likes of Willie Henderson and Jim Baxter. I was running round trying to drag the Seville players away from our own. At one stage, I had one under each arm and ended up bundling them both into the dugout. Ask any player who was there that day and they'll tell you it was one of the most incredible experiences they've ever had.

Eventually, the referee called a halt to proceedings. Whether we played the full 90 minutes or not, I'll never know, but the result certainly stood. We had a police escort to get us off the park and back to the dressing-room, although I'm not sure where the Seville constabulary had been when all hell was breaking loose just a few minutes earlier.

We were ushered up the tunnel and went to get bathed and dressed. It was like a scene from a casualty ward. Baxter had had his teeth near enough kicked out, John Greig was nursing bruises from being head-butted, Davie Wilson was struggling after being karate kicked by their keeper, and poor Bobby Shearer had scratches across his throat and ribs that were black and blue. Ronnie McKinnon did well to escape in one piece – he'd had his ear bitten during the melee.

My only wish is that there had been television cameras there to record it. If there had, it would still be watched to this day. It would be a real video nasty and I don't think people would believe what they were seeing. They talk about riots on the pitch now when there's guys trying to slap each other like a couple of girls in the playground, but this really was something to see. It was no-holds-barred stuff and it felt like it went on for an age. It took quite some time to get everyone off the pitch, almost in one piece, and to calm the situation and let the red mist lift. We'd all been absolutely astonished by what we'd been part of, but if we hadn't fought our corner we would have ended up being mauled by the Spaniards. All we did was defend ourselves and our teammates. Surely nobody would argue we didn't at least have the right to do that?

After all that had gone on in the stadium, there was the small matter of the post-match banquet to deal with. It was something of a grand tradition in European football back then, with both teams gathering after the game for a lavish celebration. It's a shame it didn't continue, because, in normal circumstances, it added to the sense of occasion. On this particular evening, quite a few of the boys weren't keen on sitting down to eat with 'the enemy', but the manager was adamant we'd go along. To say it was a tense night would be an understatement! The only consolation was that we'd won, so we could afford to be a little bit smug about that.

I've no doubt that today the match would have been abandoned, both teams would have been hauled over the coals and the media scramble would have gone on for months. As it happened, although there were pictures and reports of all that had gone on, it was pretty quickly water under the bridge and we were left to get on with preparing for the next round. The fact that we went through tells its own story. UEFA clearly didn't think we deserved to be punished, and they were quite right.

Our reward for enduring all that pain in Spain was a second-round tie against Tottenham, Jimmy Greaves and all. It was Greaves who undid us in the first game down at White Hart Lane, scoring a hat-trick as they beat us 5–2. It wasn't our finest hour and a half, and we were determined to do far better at our place.

Spurs had a good strong side – players like Dave Mackay and Danny Blanchflower in all their pomp – but we weren't short on quality either. At Ibrox, we hustled and harried for every ball and were the better side in possession too, but that man Greaves was a thorn in our side again. We went down 3–2 at home, but we got a decent press after what had been a spirited performance – far better than the London episode, that was for sure.

That turned out to be my last game in European competition, and at least it was a memorable one. I would have far preferred to have gone out on a win, but you can't always write your own script in football, and I'd had more good moments in the Continental competitions than bad ones.

The European games weren't our only ventures overseas. Foreign tours were regular and popular, and we embarked on quite a few little adventures. Going behind the Iron Curtain for a tour of the USSR in 1962 was one of the highlights, a great experience on and off the pitch.

The football was wonderful and I enjoyed the game immensely, not least because my performances were singled out for special praise. But the culture was also something to behold. Not everyone had the opportunity to venture into cities like Moscow in those days, so it was a privileged position to be in.

I have to say I abused that privilege slightly, and it almost ended up getting me thrown in jail. Taking photographs was strictly forbidden by the Communist authorities; they didn't want anything leaking into the media. As you'll see from the picture section in the middle of this book, they hadn't bargained on a bunch of canny Scots being let loose. I'd been asked if I'd smuggle a camera in and get some snaps. Being an adventurous sort, I said I'd give it a go. It didn't seem like I'd be doing any harm. Most of the pictures I have in my collection don't have me in them, since I was the official unofficial photographer, if you like. No money changed hands, but I'd come to an arrangement with one of the papers to provide images, and I sent a spool or two out by post to them during our stay. I was amazed they made it out of the country without being intercepted, but they did.

I took the camera everywhere with me, and when we were flying out of Moscow on one leg of the tour I was busy snapping away out of the plane window when I felt a firm hand on my shoulder. It was one of the minders who had been assigned to us, demanding to know what I was doing. Apparently we'd been flying over one of the military air bases when I was taking pictures, and needless to say my motives were being questioned. It took a fair bit of persuading to convince them I was entirely innocent, and there were a few fraught conversations before I was eventually allowed to disembark, a free man. Before then, they'd made sure that they'd opened the back of the camera and let light get to the film so that none of the photos could be developed, just in case I wasn't as innocent as I'd made out. I'm afraid I was no James Bond, though, just a tourist making the most of the trip.

They had their men in suits following us every step of the way. I don't think we were supposed to know they were there, but they stood out like a sore thumb and we knew we were being watched everywhere we went. It was understandable, given that we were the first football team to be invited to tour the USSR during that period.

We were looked after well, staying in the best hotels they had to offer, and made very welcome. The only stumbling block was the food, which was terrible. The culinary highlight was a consommé soup with a shelled boiled egg floating in the middle. That really was as good as it got. Everything else was verging on inedible, but we had to give it a go out of courtesy to our hosts. We understood that we were living well above the means of the average Soviet, getting the VIP treatment, so we had no reason to grumble or complain.

It is that type of experience that lives with you forever, and I know that if it hadn't been for football I wouldn't have been able to sample so many different cultures. It satisfied my wanderlust while I was still a young man, and I packed a lot into what is a relatively short career.

To see the Communist way of life was an eye-opener. When we arrived for the USSR tour, the Soviets were still basking in the glory of beating the Americans to become the first nation to get a man into space. There were exhibitions on in Moscow to mark the achievement and all manner of celebrations still going on. It was in 1961 that they'd done it, firing Major Yuri Alexeyevich Gagarin into orbit. He was more than a celebrity out there; he was treated like a god.

They'd already led the way in 1957 with *Sputnik*, the world's first man-made satellite to be successfully launched, and then with the first dog in space when wee Laika was sent up. She was almost as famous as Gagarin!

The first successful manned space mission was a momentous

event, and to be in and around the USSR at that period in time was incredible – all part of the mix of a tour that was memorable in so many ways.

In terms of the football, we started off in Moscow with a game against Lokomotiv and won 3–1. We then flew more than 1,000 miles to Georgia to take on Dinamo Tbilisi, again winning, this time by the only goal of the game, before doubling back to go and play Dinamo Kiev. Hopes of a grand slam were dashed: we drew 1–1. There was no shame in that, though, since Kiev were the Soviet champions and a very slick machine. Our previous experiences in Europe had been a major help in preparing us for the type of football we faced out there.

There was a lot of interest and intrigue surrounding our visit and the Russians turned out in great numbers to watch us train and play. Everyone was curious back home, too, with reports filtering through to keep the supporters up to date with our exploits. When we flew back to Scotland, there were thousands there to greet us. You'd think we'd won the World Cup with the welcome we received. Not that any of us were complaining; it was a very pleasant surprise.

My brush with the Russian authorities was just one of the adventures I had when we were facing European opposition. Another of my claims to fame is that I christened Hampden's floodlights in some style when Rangers played Eintracht Frankfurt in the first match at the ground played under lights. I popped up with a couple of goals, although it didn't stop us going down 3–2. Mind you, I could have got my hat-trick if the bar hadn't kept out one of my headers.

That was a so-called friendly, but, after the somewhat disappointing performance we'd put in against Eintracht in the European Cup a few years earlier, there was hunger for a spot of revenge. We didn't quite get the win we'd hoped for, but at least we proved that we could live with them after all.

We returned the favour for German opposition when we went overseas to play at the official opening of Borussia Mönchengladbach's new stadium in 1962, one of quite a few 'extra' games we played in Europe around that time. We had another trip to Russia to play Torpedo Moscow and went on a Scandinavian sojourn, with games in Denmark against Staevnet – a select team fielded by the Danes at that time – and Vejle.

Then there was the 1961 jaunt to Monte Carlo to play Monaco in the European Cup. We stayed right in the middle of town and found the time to win and lose a few shillings in the casinos. The view when you threw open the shutters in the morning was sublime, and we would quite happily have stayed there for a bit longer. Instead, we had a match to play, and we came away with a 3–2 victory to complete a very enjoyable, if somewhat brief, stay in the principality.

Each and every one of those matches added to the squad's experience, and we treated them all seriously – no question of them being some sort of holiday. What we picked up from playing so many talented sides we took into our domestic games, and there's no doubt that played a part in the success we enjoyed during that period.

17

THE TASTE OF SUCCESS

YOU WOULD THINK THAT WHEN you are involved with a big club like Rangers it might become easy to take success for granted. Hand on heart, I can say that was never the case for me or, to the best of my knowledge, any of the men I had the pleasure of playing alongside in some wonderful football teams at Ibrox.

Every trophy meant more to me than the last one. Once you've tasted the big occasion, picked up the silverware, you get an even bigger appetite to savour it again. That's what spurs you on: the desire to experience again the feeling you can only get by winning competitions.

My first involvement in a winning Rangers side was in my maiden season in the first team. After coming into the side as a deputy, first for George Young and then for Willie Logie, in 1956–57 I ended up playing out the second half of the season as the regular number 6. From January 1957 to the end of that campaign, I missed just one of the seventeen league fixtures.

What a tense finish it proved to be, as well. Hearts pushed us all the way to the finish line and were gallant challengers that year, with Celtic left in a cloud of dust, ending up down in fifth place behind Kilmarnock and Raith Rovers.

It was Hearts we had to worry about, and we knew that if we

dropped as much as a point they were waiting to pounce. We didn't, though. In the last nine games of the season, we won every single fixture, including what turned out to be the decisive game against our closest challengers at Tynecastle. Billy Simpson popped up with the only goal of the game, and we were edging closer to the prize.

There were still another four hurdles to overcome, and we did that in style, beating Airdrie, Queen's Park, Queen of the South and then, on the final day of the season, Dunfermline at East End Park to wrap up the league.

The boys had won the championship the previous year, but to retain it was special, and the celebrations were fantastic. Winning a cup is wonderful, but to go the distance over the course of a league season gives a team an extra sense of satisfaction. Nobody could dispute that we were the best in the land; the table never lies, after all.

Not only had I played my part in the first of my Rangers trophy wins, but I'd also got another feather in my cap in that first season: playing in an Old Firm derby. I made my debut in that particular fixture in the Scottish Cup, and we travelled across the city to Celtic Park. It was a baptism of fire. The tie ended up level at 4–4, and it felt like every time either team got the ball they went up the park and scored.

I remember looking around the ground and having my breath taken away. All you could see were faces, well over 55,000 of them, to be precise. It was an atmosphere like nothing I'd experienced before. If I thought that was awe-inspiring, the replay at Ibrox was something else. The official crowd figure says there were 88,000 inside Ibrox that night, but I'd bet my bottom dollar there were a few thousand unofficial supporters packed in. Unfortunately, we didn't deliver what the bulk of the crowd were hoping for, with Celtic running out 2–0 winners to put us out of the cup. I had to be content with just the one trophy win in my first season – but there would be others around the corner, even if I did have to be patient.

At least I was now a fully fledged Old Firm player. I have to admit that I didn't find those fixtures as daunting as you might imagine. I couldn't tell you exactly how many I played in, but there would have been well over 20 over the years. I loved just about every one of them, save for those when we didn't do as well as we would have liked. Fortunately, those were few and far between.

My theory on the big games was that those were the ones that were easy to play in. You had the atmosphere, the baying crowd to spur you on. You had the big-name players all over the pitch and the full glare of the media. It was show time and you had to stand up and perform.

Celtic, like Rangers, were full of some wonderful talents in that era. The Lisbon Lions were in the making, if you like, so there were a lot of up-and-coming home-grown stars to contend with. People like Billy McNeill, Jimmy Johnstone and Bertie Auld started to come into the team during my time at Ibrox, and they added a new dimension to a Celtic side that was already dangerous.

Nonetheless, I'd far rather have played in an Old Firm game every weekend than contend with some of the fixtures that we had to face. There were games where we went in as overwhelming favourites and the tension would mount if we didn't get ahead early on against teams that, in most cases, had set out to frustrate us by defending deep.

The truth was that, despite what might have been suggested in the press in the build-up to certain games against teams at the wrong end of the table, there were no easy games that I can recall. There were matches that we won well, but we were always made to work for it, and that's a different story altogether from a match somehow being 'easy'.

It was an 18-team league at that time, each side playing every other at home and away, and you rarely found clubs getting totally detached at the bottom or running away with it at the top. There wasn't the huge financial disparity between the smaller clubs and the Old Firm that there was later, so the gulf between the two big Glasgow sides and the rest wasn't as wide, and there was a real competitive edge to the league. Sides you might now consider to be less significant could pull together a talented squad. Teams like Clyde and Raith Rovers were holding their own at the top level and attracting a good standard of player year in and year out. Wouldn't it be nice to get back to the stage where there was a strong group of competitive teams?

By the time the 1957–58 season kicked off, the manager had earmarked Sammy Baird for the slot I'd been occupying. Although I started the campaign playing in the League Cup ties, Sammy eventually took over and I dropped back to the reserves for large chunks of the season, not making it into double figures for league appearances.

In saying that, I did play the bulk of the League Cup fixtures and only missed a couple of them. Unfortunately, one of those I sat out wasn't the final against Celtic. I chose a bad match to sample the cup-final experience for the first time. I was in the team that was on the receiving end of a 7–1 mauling by Celtic at Hampden in October 1957. It was a day when everything that could have gone wrong for us did, and anything that could have gone right for them did, too. It was a horrible feeling trooping off the pitch, and I was determined I'd make up for it the next time I got the chance – not realising it would be another three years before I'd get to play on the Hampden stage again.

In between, I did collect a championship medal. I was restored to the defence for the start of the 1958–59 season, and we had another humdinger of a battle with Hearts for the First Division trophy. Again, by the end of the 34 games there were only two points separating us. When we hammered them 5–0 at Ibrox in the first half of the season, with Max Murray grabbing a hat-trick and Ralph Brand getting the other two, we probably didn't realise how important the result would be.

By the time they beat us 2–0 at Tynecastle in the penultimate match of the season, it was too little too late. We even had the luxury of being able to lose the final league match of the year, at home against Aberdeen, and still win the flag.

I played in 29 out of 34 of those First Division matches, and that was the season in which I could genuinely feel like I was in with the bricks in that Scot Symon team. For the next three seasons, the only thing that kept me out of the team was the occasional injury. If I was fit, I was selected, and there was a fantastic consistency to the make-up of the team and the way we played.

We might not have won everything in sight, but we got our hands on our fair share in what was a hugely competitive era. Hearts pushed us hard and when we didn't win the league, they did, taking the title in '57–58 and then again in '59–60, as the trophy flitted between Tynecastle and Ibrox year in and year out.

That Hearts team has gone down in history as their greatest ever, and it was a formidable group of players they had, not least a forward line that always gave us a torrid afternoon. But it wasn't just them we had to contend with. Obviously, Celtic could never be discounted, even if they were struggling to mount a genuine challenge in the face of very stiff competition at that time. And the provincial sides were a real danger. Kilmarnock and Dundee FC were strong – which is borne out by the fact that they both won the First Division in the '60s, with Dundee taking it in '61–62 and Killie three years later – and they gave us a run for our money whenever we played them.

The cup competitions were highly competitive, too, and there was danger at every turn. Although I won plenty of medals with Rangers, it's the one that got away that still irks me. I played in every round of the Scottish Cup in 1959–60 as we stormed towards the final. We were expected to get the better of Berwick Rangers, Arbroath and Stenhousemuir in the early rounds, and we breezed through those ties. Then it started getting a bit trickier, with our name pulled out of the hat alongside Hibs' in the quarter-final draw. It turned out to be a classic tie at Ibrox. More than 60,000 packed in to see us beat them 3–2 to edge through.

Then came the semi-final draw – there were no hot and cold balls in the pot when they decided the ties in the last four: we were pulled out with Celtic, and we knew that if we could get the better of them we'd have one hand on the famous old trophy.

We took two attempts but got there in the end. The first tie at Hampden ended 1–1, but we cruised the replay, coming through 4–1 to set up a final showdown against a Kilmarnock side that was going for a league and cup double. They eventually lost out to Hearts in the race for the title and to us in the cup final – not that it helped me in my quest to add a Scottish Cup winner's medal to my collection.

In the semi-final against Celtic, I suffered a nasty injury. A high ball came in and I found myself jumping ahead of John Hughes, who put his knee into my back as we challenged for it. I felt the dull thud as he clattered into me and knew it wasn't good. I went down in a crumpled heap and was eventually stretchered off when they decided there was no further part for me in the game.

He'd given me a real thump and the pain kept me out of a league game down at Kilmarnock the week before we were due to play them again at Hampden, a match the boys drew 1–1. Despite my best efforts, I couldn't get fit in time for the Scottish Cup tie. I was desperate to make it, but it was obvious to everyone that I still wasn't moving freely and I had to concede defeat, albeit reluctantly.

Ian McColl came into the side in my place, Kilmarnock were

beaten 2–0 and Ian picked up a winner's medal with a sum total of one appearance in the competition that season. Little old me? I left Hampden empty-handed after playing in all six of the previous ties. Rough justice, I felt!

I didn't have to wait an awful long time to make up for that disappointment. We ended up playing Killie again in the final of the League Cup in the 1960–61 season, and I made damn sure I didn't miss a beat in that competition. Ten ties, ten games played – including the rather pleasing 7–0 semi-final stroll against poor Queen of the South at Celtic Park. The hard work had been done in the group stages, with the League Cup carrying a league format in the early weeks of the season at that stage.

Again, the draw hadn't been kind, with Celtic in our pool. We lost at home to them but made up for it with a 2–1 win in the return leg at Parkhead, when Ralphie Brand and I scored to take us through to the knockout stages. We beat Dundee over two legs in the quarter-final, then the men from Dumfries in the semi.

So it was back to Hampden and back to facing Killie. It was a bit of déjà vu, with the game ending 2–0 to us just as it had in the Scottish Cup the previous season. After the pain of losing my first cup final 7–1, and then missing what should have been my second through injury, it's fair to say nobody was happier than me when the full-time whistle sounded and we walked up to collect the trophy.

Kilmarnock must have been sick of the sight of us, to be honest. Every time they got close to winning something, they found us standing in their way. In the league that season, they were in with a real chance, and when they beat us at their place in the last month they must have thought the tide was turning their way. Then, in the last couple of weeks, we got back on track and beat Hibs and then Ayr United, thumping them 7–3 on the last day of the season to pip Killie to the title by a single point. As I say, I don't think we would have been too popular in the blue part of Ayrshire that year.

Still, it was another championship medal tucked away, making it a hat-trick in the First Division for me, and I wasn't complaining. What I desperately wanted to complete my collection was a Scottish Cup winner's medal – and I got it, in the 1961–62 season.

That year I also got my hands on the League Cup again, playing in the final against Hearts in October '61, a game we drew 1–1. When we played in the replay, almost two months later, we made sure there was clear water between us, and goals from Jimmy Millar, Ralphie Brand and Ian McMillan gave us a 3–1 win.

That fell a good few months before we were back at Hampden for the Scottish Cup final in the spring of '62. St Mirren provided the opposition. I recall they were embroiled in a real relegation scrap at the time of the cup final, but they were no pushovers. Ralph Brand and Davie Wilson undid them with a couple of goals, and 2–0 was a fair reflection of the game; we certainly deserved to win.

And that was that: I had my full collection of league, League Cup and Scottish Cup medals. It was an occasion to soak up and enjoy, not least because there was a crowd of 120,000 or so to cheer us on. Looking back, the attendances were simply phenomenal during that era. We didn't know any different at the time, but what would the players today give to turn out in front of that type of audience?

Traditionally, we would head back to the St Enoch's Hotel after a game for a post-match meal. There was no change to the routine on cup-final day. The only difference was that the meal turned into a celebration and a good time was had by all.

I remember after that St Mirren game, the doors onto the balcony were thrown open and we were able to go out and greet the large crowd of supporters that had gathered below. It was nice to be able to share it with them, given we had never had the whole open-top-bus experience. The Old Firm must be the only clubs in the world who don't get the pleasure of parading their trophies through the streets of their home city, but I can understand why that was one football ritual that never quite made it to Glasgow. You'd have people in red, white and blue cheering on one side and those in green and white throwing things at you from the other!

What I didn't realise at the time was that that evening after the game against St Mirren would prove to be my last cup-final celebration, at least as a player. When we returned to successfully defend the Scottish Cup the following season, I was a spectator, having been edged out of the team as a young upstart by the name of John Greig staked his claim. Whatever happened to him, I wonder?

I still played in a big chunk of the league games in the '62–63 title-winning campaign – 16 out of 34 of them, just short of half – so I think I'm justified in counting that as my fourth championship win with Rangers. It is the same story as with the Scottish Cup, in that I didn't get every medal I felt I deserved. The league only struck medals for 11 players, I think I'm right in saying, so they were handed out to those who'd played the most. It didn't matter how many matches you'd played, if you weren't in the top 11 on the appearance list then you didn't get a medal.

It's more than a little harsh, especially when you look at it now and every man and his dog seems to be up collecting a medal. Still, I don't think my championship-winning record was a bad return in eight years with the club. Add in a couple of League Cup successes and a Scottish Cup win, too, and I could be content with my lot.

I played a handful of games in the '63–64 season, but I wasn't getting any younger and was already looking to the future. I knew I was there in a support role that year, an old head for the youngsters to lean on when need be. I was comfortable with that;

I'd had my time, enjoyed it while it lasted and was happy to do what I could to help the next generation along the same path.

What I hadn't envisaged were the struggles that lay ahead for Rangers, for my club. I was gone by the time Celtic set off on nine-in-a-row in 1966, but I was still living and working in Glasgow, acutely aware of the pain the Ibrox support were going through. They'd been so used to success throughout the 1950s and early '60s that learning to take the rough with the smooth was never going to be easy. Still, they stuck with their team through thick and thin. Not that I would have expected anything less – they'd always backed our team to the hilt. You maybe don't hear individual shouts or chants when you're out on that pitch, but you certainly hear the roar that the Ibrox crowd generates. If that doesn't inspire you, nothing ever will. It was an honour and a privilege to spend a good part of my working life as a football player with a Rangers jersey on my back.

18

SLIM PICKINGS

AN HONOUR AND A PRIVILEGE: those were the words I used to describe how I felt about playing for Rangers Football Club, that grand old institution. You would think everyone who got the chance to pull on a light-blue jersey would feel the same sense of pride – but you would be wrong.

There was one in particular who made no secret of the fact he didn't really give a damn about the club, the team or anyone but himself. Step forward, Mr Jim Baxter. Now, at this point I have to make a qualification. Jim Baxter was an exceptional football talent, a man blessed with incredible skill and vision, and one who, for many supporters who paid their money at the Ibrox gate, is a hero, a legend and an icon all rolled into one.

But should all of that mean he's above criticism? Not for me, it doesn't. I've always called a spade a spade, and in this case I'm not saying anything now that I didn't say to Jim's face when he was alive. He knew exactly how I felt about the way he treated the club and his teammates.

As I say, I would never decry the man's skill with a ball at his feet. The problem was he didn't make the best of that gift – he wasted it. People talk about the great games Baxter played and the wonderful performances he gave. What they don't mention are the many indifferent displays when he simply couldn't be bothered trying a leg. For the rest of us, busting a gut for the team, that type of attitude stuck in the throat.

Another galling thing was that the treatment Jim received from the manager, Scot Symon, was always superior to that which the rest of the boys got. It was as though he had a hold over him. He was always softer on him than he was on the others, and that didn't go down well. Everyone else called him 'the Boss' and stood to attention when he was in the room or on the training field; not our Jim, though. But he got away with it, time and time again.

I can remember one incident, at Stirling Albion, when, as usual, some bastard tried to nail me on the pitch. I tackled him fair and square, winning the ball no questions asked, but when I was on the ground he planted his studs into the back of my hand. I got up and saw him smiling at me, so I sorted him out. He went down screaming. The ball was away at the other end, taking the referee with it, so I got away with it.

When I was going for a bath after the match, Scot Symon came in and roared, 'Davis, I saw that. What do you think you were doing?' Like a fool, I rose to the bait. 'They tell me you were no angel when you played either,' I said.

He couldn't speak, he was that angry. His face went red like a beetroot and he was shaking with rage. All he could do was shake his head, growl and walk away. It won me a few votes with the rest of the lads, because he was a bit of a tyrant; what he said was gospel – no arguments. The Boss, as he'll always be to me, was big on discipline and an old-school character. Even by the time his reign was coming to an end, his ways were becoming a bit antiquated as the game changed and the approach to man-management softened. The arm-around-the-shoulder approach was alien to Symon and his generation, but the next wave of managers began to realise that different players responded to different treatment. For the Boss, it was hard line, and if you veered off course you soon knew about it.

The point is he would be quick enough to pull me up for anything and everything, yet Baxter was above the law, so to speak. He could do anything he liked on or off the pitch and never face any consequences or get a dressing-down. Symon would never speak to Jim the way he spoke to me or the others, and that was detrimental in the dressing-room. The rest of the side didn't like the way Baxter disrespected the club and his team by not pulling his weight, yet he got away scot-free every time.

Once a Ranger, always a Ranger – that was the motto we lived by. For Jim, though, that didn't seem to apply. It didn't feel like he cared about the club, only himself. That was the arrogance of the man.

If you don't believe me, let me quote you a few brief extracts from his own book *Baxter: The Party's Over* and you can make up your own mind. For example, '*Perhaps I did enjoy myself too much, but what's too much? Moderation, as far as I'm concerned, is for moderate people. Half-measures are for little people.*'

Now, call me sensitive if you like, but I always believed in looking after myself and viewed moderation as part and parcel of life as a professional sportsman. Applying Jim's logic, that makes me one of life's little people – and I'm sorry, I don't take kindly to that assertion. I shared a dressing-room with him, after all, and if he classed himself a bigger man than me or any of the other dedicated professionals he appeared to be sneering at, I'd happily argue against him any day of the week.

On the subject of pay, having left to double his weekly wage from £22 per week at Rangers to £45 at Sunderland, Jim noted: '*By tradition, it was the responsibility of the captain to transmit any dressing-room grievances to the boardroom, but wee Bobby Shearer wasn't interested in the responsibility. Bobby was a great Ranger. He would have played for nothing, I'm sure. So he wouldn't protest on our*

*behalf. "Well, Bobby," I'd say to him, "if you won't go upstairs, I will."
... I was very fond of him and still am. But all the loyalty and the
gung-ho stuff, while sounding good, didn't pay the rent.'*

Jim's right: Bobby Shearer would have played for nothing. If
that makes him a bad person, so be it. Bobby was Rangers through
and through; cut him and he'd bleed blue. If he wasn't prepared to
be Jim's gofer, it was for all the right reasons. Like the rest of us,
he saw the effort, or lack of it, that the man put in on the training
field and could make his own judgement as to whether he should
be banging down the manager's door demanding a pay rise for
him. If Baxter thought that was somehow down to a lack of
courage, he was a poor judge of character. Bobby had guts and
determination by the bucketful. Nothing scared the man. And
yes, he was fiercely loyal to Rangers Football Club – to try to use
that as some form of criticism just seems warped.

'I don't blame myself for some of the liberties I took with Rangers.'
There, in a nutshell, is the problem. To take liberties with the
club, with any club, is an insult to your manager, your fellow
players and, far more importantly, the supporters who pay their
hard-earned money at the turnstile to watch week in and week
out.

*'The truth is that any star – and I was a star by this time – can get
away with murder. On one condition – he has to balance it all up as
soon as he steps out onto that football park.'* Only he didn't balance it
up, not often enough, at least. The bad or average games far
outweighed the exceptional ones, as far as I'm concerned. There
were far too many occasions when the effort and application just
weren't there and lot of that was down to him getting away with
'murder' through the week. He'd roll into training still half-cut
from the night before; on occasion, he'd turn up for matches the
worse for wear too. To me, that was just taking the rise out of the
hard-working professionals he shared a dressing-room with, and I
just couldn't stomach it.

Nowadays, we look at Lionel Messi and marvel at his sublime skill – the best in the world, they say, and one of the best of all time. Do you think he's out on the town the night before a game? Not a chance. All you ever read about is how dedicated Messi is and the effort he puts in on the training field every day of his life. When he plays a match, nobody covers more ground, whether it's with the ball or trying to win it back. That's what makes him special. Jim Baxter, on the other hand, thought he was above the type of hard graft that Lionel Messi doesn't seem to have an issue with.

'*Training was, however, something of a problem for me.*' I guess honesty is always the best policy, even if 'something of a problem' is a touch of an understatement. Jim felt he was too good to work hard, that somehow he could survive on ability alone. If that had been the case, he would have played for five or ten years longer than he did. He should have been gracing football pitches long after the time when he retired, but he ended up washed-up far too soon. He always maintained he had no regrets, but I can't help but wonder whether in quieter moments he looked back and thought what might have been if only he'd done things differently.

'*Davie Kinnear was the Ibrox trainer, and clashes and quarrels were inevitable . . . It might have been slightly different if I had had genuine respect for his training methods. I had none.*' Respect. That was the problem. Jim didn't respect anyone or anything, as far as I could see. Even Scot Symon, a man he professed great affection for, was treated shoddily in that his star man refused to give his all for him.

Naturally, given our background, I had an awful lot of time for Davie Kinnear and knew from personal experience how skilled he was at his job. If it wasn't for Davie, I would never have kicked a ball for Rangers, and if Jim had given him half a chance, he would have been fitter and stronger than he'd ever been in his life. He didn't give him a chance, and he lost out because of it.

It wasn't just people that Jim refused to show any respect for, it applied to Rangers Football Club and it applied to the British Army too. As you'll understand, we were poles apart on that front. *'Ironically, I had hardly stepped inside the door at Ibrox – in July 1960 – when the British Army knocked at my own door . . . Now a lot of people will tell you that conscription and the Army was a marvellous experience, something not to be missed, makes a man of you, all that sort of bull. Personally, I found it was almost a total waste of time.'*

I'm one of those people Jim's accusing of spinning some 'bull', as he puts it. As far as I'm concerned, the Army does make a man of you; it is a life-changing experience. The Black Watch, with whom he also served, is the greatest regiment in the world as far as I'm concerned, and has given wonderful opportunities to so many men. For Jim to class that as a waste of time points to someone who went in with the wrong attitude in the first place, which doesn't surprise me when it comes to Mr Baxter.

I also take offence at the suggestion he goes on to make, which is that Rangers worked the system, 'pulling strings' to keep him close to Glasgow and still in the team. That feeds into a myth that has been perpetuated down through the years – that Rangers used their influence to ensure that their players had an easy time of it when serving in the armed forces – one that's a slur on all of the Ibrox men who have served their country with distinction in almost every conflict since the Great War. Try telling Willie Thornton, a Military Medal winner after his heroics in Sicily in the Second World War, or Ian McPherson, a Distinguished Flying Cross recipient in the same war, that their club was playing a game when it came to military service.

What I do know from my own experience is that footballers did get special treatment, different opportunities from normal conscripts, but that was across the board. I was a humble East Fife player when I was given the option of body-swerving active service in Korea, but I chose not to. What I'm saying is that the assertion that it was a Rangers tactic to get players 'off the hook' when it came to army duty is just wrong. Too many men served on front lines in all corners of the world to suggest that.

'*In the noble cause of showing the flag, the Army sent a team of professional footballers – all conscripts of course – on a seven-week tour of the Far East . . . And don't imagine for a moment that we were staying in Army huts. Nothing like that for Baxter and his mates. Certainly not. This was five-star hotel stuff all the way . . .*'

I lived in army huts, in a tiny hooch with mortars flying overhead. It makes my blood boil to think others who wore the uniform of the British Army did it with such disdain and disrespect to colleagues who dodged bullets. By all means, if you are invited to represent the forces in a sporting capacity, I've got no quarrel with that – but at least do it with a touch of humility and understanding of the sacrifices that other soldiers and their families make.

I made the decision to go out to Korea and fight for my country, I have lived with the consequences every day of my life since and did so while sharing a dressing-room with Baxter. It wasn't something he would ever comprehend, even if he did have kind words to say about me: '*On the football field, opponents bounced off Harry, although that's not to say he couldn't play the game. When he tackled, he seldom missed, and he was a better passer of the ball than he was usually given credit for.*'

Maybe Mr Baxter did speak sense after all . . . I'd wholeheartedly endorse his assessment of my own qualities! In all seriousness, my relationship with Jim was a complex one in many respects. I got on well with him, but he knew exactly what I thought of him and his ways, if that makes sense. He was aware of his own failings, you have to credit him with that, but what I could never accept was his apparent delight in his misdemeanours, especially when they were at the expense of other people who would stick their neck on the line for him.

The thing is, we all knew what he was capable of, even before he joined us. For all I have a reputation as a hard man, I have only ever gone out on a football field with the intention of harming an opponent on one occasion. That player was Jim Baxter.

It was one Saturday when we were going across to Fife to play Raith Rovers. Jim was their star man and it was already being widely rumoured that he might be coming west to join us. Before the game, the boys singled him out as the one who could do us real damage, and they said it was up to me to sort him out. The added incentive was that he was due to replace Willie Stevenson, a very popular player in our squad. So I did. Early in the game, I went crunching into a tackle with Jim, taking him clean out. He took no further part in proceedings and wasn't around to work his magic on us.

I don't look back on that particular incident with any great pride; it was just part and parcel of the game. I didn't make a habit of it, that's for sure. I apologised to him later and he accepted it. I wasn't the first and certainly wouldn't be the last to dish it out, and players of Jim's ilk had to learn to take it.

As I say, I got on fine with him – mainly because he failed to take on board any of the criticism levelled at him. If he'd taken some of the things I said or did to heart, we'd be sworn enemies, but to him it was like it was all a big joke. It was so infuriating that I admit I did get physical with him on occasion, to try to bring him back into line. The most notorious of those incidents has grown into something of an urban myth. The story goes that I hung Jim on a dressing-room peg at Ibrox and left him there after he pushed me too far. The reality is close, but it didn't quite happen like that.

Basically, he had come in on the morning of the game pissed out of his mind. Most of the boys had had it up to the eyeballs with him and the way he was behaving, but nobody really bothered to say anything. It was a waste of breath and energy. But I couldn't let it go; it wasn't in my nature. So I laid my hands on the chest of his jersey and lifted him clean off the floor, his legs dangling as if he were a puppy being lifted by the scruff of its neck. I held him there for a while, staring him in the eye, showed him the pegs along the wall and told him in no uncertain terms that if he didn't buck his ideas up I'd string him up there and leave him. I never actually did it, contrary to what some of the boys might suggest. I could have, mind you, and maybe I should have!

That story has been retold by others a thousand times, and it's grown arms and legs along the way. I think in some accounts I am said to have left him hanging there for a week. But there's at least a bit of truth to it all.

That was just one instance. There were plenty of others along the way. I can remember walking up the tunnel at half-time on another one of Jim's many 'off days'. He'd been out there basically walking around while the rest of us were breaking sweat trying to carry him as a passenger. I heard him saying to Willie Henderson, his best pal, that without the two of them the team was garbage – or words to that effect, if a little more colourful than that. Again, I couldn't let it pass. I collared him and asked him what he was saying. 'Nothing, Harry, honest.' He wouldn't say it to my face but I'd heard all I needed to. He just didn't give a damn about the rest of us and no doubt believed the rubbish he was spouting. He was playing in Rangers teams packed full of international players, yet somehow it was all a bit beneath him.

Yet still we persevered because we knew underneath it all was a sublime footballer who could turn a match on its head with one flick of his boot. The manager wanted to build his team with Baxter at the heart of it, and everything was geared towards getting him on the ball at every opportunity. Wherever he was on the park, he was the one we had to look to with our passes.

Scot Symon's big mantra for me and the other defenders was 'Win the ball and pass it to Jim, win the ball and pass it to Jim.'

The problem was, if Jim wasn't interested you just ended up playing yourself into trouble. There was one game when I was on the ball and turned it square to pass it to Baxter. I then turned half away to carry on my run and the bugger passed it straight back, knowing fine well I'd no chance of getting to it. He just looked at me and laughed. It was five minutes before half-time and when I came off for the break I was still absolutely livid. I near enough sprinted up the tunnel to catch him in the dressing-room and grabbed him by the throat. I told him in no uncertain terms that if he did that to me again he wouldn't be playing the next week . . . or the week after that. All he could muster was 'Oh, Harry, come on.'

He just didn't take offence; he couldn't take anything seriously. For all his bravado, he wasn't a big lad, and Jim knew he couldn't fight back. That little episode had a short-term effect, but nothing would change him in the long term.

It was the same on and off the park. I'll always remember being invited along to a house party in Glasgow, a nice, civilised affair with just a few people having some quiet drinks. Nothing out of the ordinary, until Jim Baxter and his cronies arrived at the door trying to cause a scene.

He didn't know I was inside and he was on the doorstep with a couple of the Celtic first-team players, pestering folk to be let inside to join the party. I listened from inside as he got louder and louder. He was used to getting his own way, particularly if there was a drink to be had. Eventually, I stepped forward and stood in the doorway. The look on his face when he saw me was a picture. I gently suggested he turn away and leave us all in peace, and reluctantly he got the message. It was probably the first and only time he'd ever missed out on a party, and I think that would have hurt him more than losing any football match.

That sums him up, really. It wasn't about Rangers or about the sport. It was all about what being involved in the game could do for him off the park. That became the main focus in life. The party lifestyle took hold, along with the gambling, and football seemed to fall pretty far down the list of priorities.

I wish I could have got through to him, have put him on the straight and narrow. But it was one battle I was never going to win, no matter how hard I tried. Jim Baxter will always be remembered as one of the great football talents Scotland has ever produced, but I for one simply cannot overlook the contempt with which he treated his club and his teammates. Too often we slip on the rose-tinted glasses and let nostalgia take over. The reality doesn't always match the nostalgic picture that can be painted, and with regard to Jim Baxter I'm afraid that is the case.

19

THE IRON MAN

MY CONFRONTATIONS WITH JIM BAXTER were, in all honesty, the exception rather than the rule. I did not go through my life picking fights with people; I did not enjoy throwing my weight around. The other thing I did not do was suffer fools gladly or enjoy losing, and on occasion those two factors led me to be what I would class as 'robust' in my approach.

I have been described by some as a hard man on the pitch and a gentleman off it. I am happy enough to accept that. I hope it's an accurate reflection of the way I have always tried to conduct myself.

For people who don't know me, there can be a tendency for my reputation to cloud their judgement. From very early in my football career, within months of playing my first game for the top team at Ibrox, I was labelled with the 'Iron Man' tag by the newspapers. It was one that stuck with the supporters, too.

There's no doubt I was a rugged player. I was there to add a bit of steel to the team, with the Boss making sure there was a very good blend right through the side. Eric Caldow was a fast, sharp and quick-witted player; Bobby Shearer, or 'Captain Cutlass' as he was to a generation, was hard as nails. It was the same all over the pitch, with steel and silk in equal measure. Nobody can argue that it didn't work, and I don't think that has changed to this day: the greatest modern teams have players who are prepared to dig in and battle. You can't play the game if you don't have the ball, and at the highest level you only get it by going out and winning it.

Getting hold of the ball was what I was sent out there for, and, like everything I do in life, I didn't do half measures. I was never a dirty player, never late with a tackle, but if there was a tackle there to be won I'd make sure it was me who came out on top.

If I did clatter some guys, it was usually because they had set out to do me first. Because my reputation preceded me, I put up with a lot. There would be studs going into my hand while I was on the ground, or a boot being stamped on my neck while I was down. If that happened, I would make sure they knew not to try it a second time. But I never went on the field with the intention of doing harm to anyone, or at least only once – as I mentioned earlier.

Usually, I would act only in self-defence, or at least in the defence of my teammates. It got me into a few scrapes, right enough, quite often when we were playing Continental teams who had their own line in dirty tricks.

One of the bizarre European experiences came against Anderlecht in 1959. They had a forward called Joseph Jurion, who was needling me off the ball right the way through the game. He was another who decided to go for the old studs-in-the-hands trick while I was on the ground towards the end of the game.

That was the straw that broke the camel's back, and I got right onto my feet and sprinted off after him. The red mist was down. The crowd had seen my reaction and were roaring me on. Fortunately, there was enough open space between us that by the time I got near, I'd started to see the funny side of the crowd's reaction, and I couldn't go through with it. Lucky for him, and probably lucky for me!

In that same tie against Anderlecht, another of their players had caught me for the umpteenth time in the game and I cracked. I walloped him one on the nose, doing real damage. In an instant, I was flooded with remorse. When we played the return match, great play was made of getting the two of us together, and he accepted my apologies. He also said he wouldn't make the same mistake again.

Of course, there was also the Battle of Seville and all that went on there, and countless other run-ins I had up and down the country over the years. But I always maintained I had more to offer than just my defensive qualities, and that was something of which I tried to convince the Boss on more than one occasion.

Jimmy Millar and Ralph Brand approached me one day and said they were going to get permission to stay behind and practise some movements after training. I was part of the same 'triangle' with them on the pitch, so it made sense for me to work with them after hours and build on what was already a good understanding we had struck up. The longer you play with the same players, the better you get at reading their movements and passes – and we had plenty of time to get acquainted, playing hundreds of games together.

It was good of them to invite me to join them in their overtime, and I didn't hesitate. I loved playing the game, loved training and would never complain about spending an extra hour on the pitch.

We were about half an hour into our little session when a booming voice came hollering out of the stand: 'Davis, come here.' It was Mr Symon, clearly none too happy. He shouted, 'What the heck [he didn't swear] do you think you're doing?'

When I explained to him that I'd stayed back for a bit of extra work, to do some passing and moving exercises with Jimmy and Ralphie, I thought he'd be delighted. Not a bit of it. If anything, he got even angrier. He snapped, 'I don't want you to be a ball-player. You are a ball-winner. That's why I like you. Get in there, have a bath and go home.'

And that was that, the end of my self-improvement scheme. As funny as it sounds, looking back on it now, I was actually a bit upset by that little episode. I knew that people perceived me as a destroyer, but I liked to think I had more to my game than solely that.

When I started out in football, I did so as a centre-forward, an out-and-out attacker with a good nose for goal and, I'd like to think, a decent set of skills to go with my power and pace. Over time, it was my defensive qualities that came to the fore, but I knew my way around a football pitch and never stopped wanting to improve. It's just a shame that the boss didn't necessarily see it the same way.

Despite his protestations, I did actually get to play a bit of football in my many years with Rangers. When you're surrounded by good players who want to get the ball down and do things the right way, everyone feeds off one another.

No matter what our specific job in the team was, the common bond was a work ethic and a fitness that developed under Davie Kinnear's coaching. Given the head start I'd had during my rehabilitation, I don't think there was anyone fitter than me during my eight years at Ibrox. After everything my body had been through, I knew the importance of keeping myself strong, and the only way to do that was with sheer hard work, nothing else.

I used to come off at the end of the game and if I wasn't tired, I wasn't happy. I'd ask the same of my teammates, driving them on, and we had some relentless characters in that side. Bobby Shearer would run his heart out for Rangers and there were many of the same ilk.

That's not to say we were always one big happy family. There were ups and downs along the way, but we'd always get back on an even keel. I took it upon myself to look after the youngsters at the club. If anyone was in trouble, they'd look to me to sort it out.

Boys like Alex Willoughby and Jim Forrest would let me know if they were getting stick from the older players and knew I'd take care of them. I didn't like bullies, and unfortunately football's like every other walk of life – you find them every now and again. I wouldn't stand for it at any of the clubs I was involved with, and most people appreciated that.

The one type of person I loathe perhaps even more than a bully is a cheat. It wasn't something that was common when I was playing, but I see it in just about every game I watch now. Diving, simulation . . . label it what you like, I'll stick to calling it cheating. There's far too much of it going on and we're in grave danger of football becoming a non-contact sport.

It is making the job of the referee almost impossible. They are left in a no-win situation. If they don't give the penalty and get it wrong, they take pelters; if they do give the penalty and they've got it wrong, they take pelters. If they followed the letter of the law, they'd be issuing yellow cards for simulation left, right and centre, and we'd end up with certain players getting sent off more often than not. Then the referee would get it in the neck again, because the game would be ruined as a spectacle if one team was down to ten or nine men – not what the paying public want to see.

So sending them off isn't the solution, but I would like to see far more being done in terms of looking back over game footage and punishing the offenders. Maybe then the message would start to get through.

I'm writing this having just watched an Old Firm game that should have been a wonderful spectacle and was in many ways, the first to be played after Rangers had gone into administration. Ibrox was packed, the crowd was hyped up and there were plenty of goals. Rangers might have won 3–2, but there were three red cards that afternoon, and I can't help but think that spoils the game. People pay their money to see 22 players on the park, but very rarely do they get that in the big games.

Why don't we just agree it is time to bring in video technology and move on? If it works in cricket, tennis and every other sport you could care to mention, why not football? It would at least help the referees make better and more consistent decisions and avoid them being conned by players trying to gain an unfair advantage.

Apart from the fact that it is putting a real dampener on games – we seem to spend more time talking about controversial decisions than the actual football – it is also setting a terrible example for the next generation. Players have to realise that every time they take a dive, there's a young kid sitting somewhere at home who watches it on television and then goes out into the playground or onto the playing field and attempts to replicate it. Kids need to learn to take the rough and tumble that football brings. If they grow up thinking that you go down every time you're so much as touched, we're storing up big trouble for the future. You wait and see – the Iron Man is fast becoming a thing of the past.

20

MOVING ON

HOW DO YOU KNOW WHEN it is time to give up? It's the age-old question that every football player has to face eventually. Some make the decision early, some leave it late and others have it made for them.

In my case, it was a bit of both, because after I'd made the decision to hang up my boots I was tempted to give it another go, to see if the old legs would soldier on for an extra season or two.

I was 31 when I left Rangers in the summer of 1964. That sounds like I was still in my prime, but at that stage I would have been classed a veteran. You have to remember the pitches were heavy, the balls were heavy, the boots were heavy ... all of that combined ensured the shelf life of the average player was far shorter than it would be in today's game, with the improvements in conditions and equipment. The other factor was that I relied heavily on my pace, strength and stamina – all things that you can't hold on to forever, no matter how hard you train.

I'd been fortunate to have steered clear of serious injury during my eight years at Ibrox, although playing on through the pain barrier wasn't uncommon, and you had to quickly accept that many injuries would not have time to be repaired or fix themselves before the next match. That's when good relationships with the doctor and physio came into their own. I got the very best of treatment during occasional spells of injury and was fortunate that when it was time to lie on the treatment table I was sure they would go the extra mile to keep me on the right road. So they did, with my body being patched up plenty of times during my playing days with Rangers. The work that had been done by the medical staff always proved to be spot on. The staff, particularly Davie Kinnear, knew the peculiarities of my own situation – I'd had 18 operations in my lower stomach area alone, after all – and tailored the treatment and training to me where possible.

To have played on into my 30s when I'd been told when I was still a young man that I'd never kick a ball in anger was an achievement in itself. So the fact I'd had eight great years softened the blow of realising that Father Time was creeping up on me.

Of course, it was a huge wrench to face leaving Rangers, but I was prepared for it. For a couple of seasons, I'd been expecting to be pulled upstairs and told that my contract wouldn't be renewed, but I'd been pleasantly surprised when I'd been offered new deals. Eventually, though, the inevitable happened and it was broken to me that there wouldn't be another contract. It was time to move on, to pull the curtain down on that chapter in my life.

I was all set to call it a day, and I had the chance to do some coaching work at Rangers, but Willie Thornton nipped in and persuaded me to carry on playing for a bit longer with him at Partick. At the back of my mind, I felt my sharpness was fading and I'd lost half a yard of pace. I was facing a bit of a dilemma. Obviously, Willie was Mr Rangers; he was held in very high regard at Ibrox well after he had left to embark on his managerial career with Dundee and then Partick. I had tremendous respect for him and didn't want to let him down, even though, in my heart of hearts, I knew it was time to hang up the boots.

Willie had taken over at Firhill following David Meiklejohn's death in 1959, so by the time I arrived he was very well established.

He had succeeded in keeping Thistle safe and secure in the First Division, even if they were struggling for money at that stage and it was a bit of a rag-tag team that Willie was having to put together.

Two seasons before I arrived, he'd taken Thistle as high as third in the league, so by no means were they perennial strugglers, and everyone could see the good job he was doing. They came close to being runners-up to us in that 1962–63 season, finishing just a couple of points behind Hearts, and for Willie to take his side above Celtic and become Glasgow's 'second team' was a feather in his cap.

Willie was such a calming figure and that was obviously appreciated by the Partick directors. When he asked me to sign for Partick, I could easily have said no, but part of me wondered if I'd regret retiring when I still had the option of playing on. Plus, everyone who's spent time in Glasgow develops a bit of a soft spot for Thistle; they're just one of those teams.

The other factor was that it was the chance to keep earning from the game for at least another year, something that couldn't be overlooked. I didn't go into it looking any further than a single season, but it gave me a bit more breathing space as I came to consider life after Rangers.

When I stopped playing at Ibrox, I was earning £30 per week, only £7 or £8 more than the average working man at that stage. It was still a good living wage, but it wasn't a king's ransom that meant we could live happily ever after. All of us players knew we had to keep working in some capacity once the football was over. It frustrates me to see the money swilling around in the game now, especially because I watched some of the great names in the game struggle after they left Ibrox.

I count myself fortunate that I was able to carve out a new career and make a decent living – a second life, if you like. Others didn't have that opportunity, and I'll never forget bumping into

George Young at a game when he was in his later years, confined to a wheelchair and unrecognisable from the giant of a man who had patrolled Scotland's football pitches with such aplomb. It turned out he was living in a single-end flat in Grangemouth, struggling to get by. A man who captained his club and country with distinction was forgotten once he was past his sell-by date, cast aside without the cushion of the millions that somebody of his stature could expect to have earned today.

People may argue that players had a duty to take care of themselves, to plan for the future and invest in pensions. Maybe there's an element of truth in that, but I would suggest that the wages my peers and I received didn't leave the luxury of being able to squirrel money away for a rainy day. We all had to work in the real world after we finished playing, and I only wish the players today would appreciate the privileges they enjoy and the opportunities they have in front of them. I don't begrudge them it in the slightest, but it pains me to hear players complaining of being tired or having to play too many games. They are richly rewarded and have to be willing to roll up the sleeves and earn that money.

For me, the move to Partick kept some money coming in, and I also got to keep playing the game I loved. If the truth be told, it wasn't the best period in my career, and I started to be troubled with the types of niggling injuries you can expect when you hit a certain age. Again, it was nothing serious, but it was enough to keep me out of a few games here and there while I was patched up ready for action again.

It was the Rangers old boy network that had engineered my move across the city to the Jags. When Scot Symon decided I wasn't getting a new deal at Ibrox, he tipped Willie Thornton the wink and alerted him to my impending availability. I dare say that Willie probably knew before I did that I'd be looking for a new club that summer! He stepped in once it was all official and was the first out of the blocks. I'm sure if I'd waited there would have been other possibilities to consider, but I was quite happy to go to Partick.

We actually had a decent season. The objective was to make sure we were safe in the First Division, and we achieved that comfortably, picking up at least a point in the majority of games over the course of the year.

Thistle at that stage hadn't become the sort of yo-yo team that we tend to think of them as now, popping up with a promotion now and again before drifting back down to the lower leagues. When I joined, they'd been in the top league since the turn of the century and were mainstays of the First Division, expected to prove a thorn, or thistle, in the side of the big teams when they came calling at Maryhill.

I did what I could to help maintain that tradition, and we ended up finishing 11th in the 18-team league, well away from the relegation zone but not threatening to repeat the third-place finish of a couple of years previously. There were some decent results along the way, and we seemed to be able to raise our game for the big ones. I remember drawing 1–1 with Rangers at Firhill, much to everyone in the blue half of Glasgow's disappointment.

We deserved it, though, and I was quite chuffed. I went in, got dressed and was walking down the street outside the ground when a Rolls-Royce pulled up. John Lawrence, the Rangers chairman, got out of the car. He said, 'Hello there, Harold. You played well today. Nasty, though, taking a point from us.' I thought, 'Here we go, a dressing-down from the boss.' Instead, he went on to thank me for what I'd done when I was at Ibrox and told me that if I ever fancied a cast down on his estate I was welcome to fish his hill lochs. I'd done that a few times while I was on the books at Ibrox, and he said that simply because we'd parted company it didn't mean I couldn't carry on as before.

Usually, he didn't stop to speak to anyone, so it was a lovely gesture, and I took up his invitation and headed down two or three times. His estate was only 45 minutes from Glasgow, but it felt like a world away, set in wonderful rolling countryside and totally secluded. He'd worked hard to build up his empire and he'd got his rewards; you couldn't begrudge him that.

If you've ever been to Firhill, you know what it's like, with tight streets all about and supporters milling around at full-time. When Rangers were over to play, it was busier than usual and the road was absolutely mobbed with fans standing around chewing the fat or making their way back home. Mr Lawrence took a bit of flak from supporters even in the time he was standing in the street talking to me, so I appreciated him taking time out to do that.

It reinforced the message that once you've been a Ranger, you're always a Ranger. The club looks after you when you're there, but it doesn't end when you walk out the front door. It gets under your skin and there's always that link.

The chairman at that time was a figurehead and commanded respect. This was long before football clubs got mixed up in the stock market or started borrowing millions from the banks. It was far simpler that way. If something had to be sorted, it was done by the manager and the chairman, no middlemen or agents and no messing around. I shudder when I see the mess the club has been in during recent years and can't help but wonder why it was allowed to get that bad. If only they could rewind and go back to the days when the club was run as a tight ship, none of it would have happened. We were well looked after – we had the best suits, stayed in the best hotels – but the money wasn't flashed around. Wages were good but by no means excessive. I don't think anyone from my era got rich from the game, that's for sure, but that structure ensured the club thrived.

As it happened, I almost didn't play in that game against Rangers, as I'd been struggling with a leg injury in the build-up to it. I'd pulled a muscle in a game against Celtic a couple of weeks earlier, and these things were taking longer to heal than when I was a young man.

It was typical of the type of problem I'd had through that season, and when it came to the end of the season Willie Thornton and I agreed it would be best to call it a day. I'd squeezed the extra year out of my old body and enough was enough – time to move on. When we'd initially sat down to discuss my move from Rangers, he'd asked me to give it just 12 more months. I'd kept my side of the bargain and thought I'd timed it about right to take a breather.

I'd made it clear I was keen on coaching, and I was aware of an opportunity that was just perfect for me. Many of my peers from my Rangers days were starting out on coaching careers too, and it was a natural progression for us after our excellent schooling in winning ways at Ibrox. My old colleagues and I would end up crossing paths quite a few times in the years ahead as the guard changed and we took over from the older generation.

At around the same time as my old friend and teammate Bobby Shearer was preparing to cut his teeth with Queen of the South, I was about to get a chance with the other football royalty: Queen's Park.

21

BY ROYAL APPOINTMENT

LONG BEFORE I HAD KICKED my last ball as a professional player, the move into coaching had been in my thoughts. The possibility of getting involved at Ibrox under Scot Symon had been mentioned, but deep down I harboured the ambition of standing on my own two feet as a manager in my own right.

Getting that opportunity was not a given by any stretch of the imagination. I had a good playing pedigree and strong contacts by virtue of my length of service at Rangers, but a chairman or board of directors would still need to take a chance on a young man with no previous experience.

It transpired that it wasn't a chairman or directors who gave me that opportunity, it was the committee of Queen's Park. It is such a unique and wonderful club in so many ways, and if I had been able to hand-pick the team with which I would embark on my coaching career I could have done no better than to choose the Spiders.

My retirement coincided with their search for a new coach, and it was suggested to me that I should apply. I did, and they were interested in listening to what I had to say. Once I'd spoken to them, I was offered the job and didn't hesitate to accept.

Their amateur status made Queen's a one-off in the senior

game. That brought challenges for the managers who led the team, with a different pool of players to choose from by virtue of the inability to pay wages, but it also created a spirit that I have never seen replicated. Every single person on that pitch was there for the love of the game and because they wanted to play for the club, not for a pay packet. You quite literally couldn't buy what we had.

I arrived at the club in the summer of 1965 and to say I had a hard act to follow would be an understatement. But then I always liked a challenge. The vacancy at Hampden had arisen because of Eddie Turnbull's decision to leave and take over at Aberdeen – a huge break for Eddie, and one he made the very best of. The success he went on to have at Pittodrie and also with Hibs is well documented, but he had learned his trade at Queen's Park, and I saw it as a chance to do the same thing.

Living in Glasgow and being so involved in football, I was already part of the social circle at Queen's prior to the vacancy coming up. I was one of the boys, if you like, and they were a great bunch of people. Perhaps that helped my case when they came looking for a new manager. I was already well known at the club. Even so, I had to put my serious face on once I was in the post and make sure I drew a line between the business side of what we were doing on the pitch and the pleasurable side of the camaraderie that there was at the club. I think I managed to strike that balance pretty well.

When I was approached and asked to take on the job, I didn't have to give it serious consideration. It was right for me on so many levels: it was in Glasgow, it was a well-run club with potential and I knew the squad well.

Under Eddie, the team had finished fourth in the Second Division in the 1964–65 season, a couple of places short of promotion to the big league. They had spent a few years up in the First Division while I was at Rangers, in the late 1950s, but the challenge to get back up among the top teams was huge. That was another of the big attractions.

There were other fringe benefits, too, as far as I was concerned. It was a part-time job, which suited me fine. I'd go up to a loch and do a bit of fishing in the morning and then head to the ground at 2 p.m. and work through to 9 p.m. The job came with a house attached, as many managers' posts did in those days. Having spent our time in Glasgow living in the shadow of Ibrox, the family and I upped sticks and shifted to Mount Florida. We were very well looked after, put up in a lovely sandstone villa just a stone's throw from the ground.

It's easy to forget how Hampden used to look, before it got its modern makeover, but in those days it was a far more earthy environment for football. It was a big old bowl with terraces that seemed to go on forever. The pitch, as you'd expect at the national stadium, was lovingly tended to, and I do think it was to our advantage having that as our home ground. You could argue that having a few thousand fans rattling around in Hampden isn't great for creating an atmosphere, but the prestige and thrill of playing in those surroundings more than made up for it. Opposition teams loved to come and play us on our patch, but more than anything our players thrived on getting to run out on that famous turf every second week. It's the home of football in this country, and if you can't be inspired by working there then nothing will motivate you. I know it certainly put a spring in my step to walk out the gate of the house each day and head for my 'office' across the road.

I had a busy working schedule, even if it was technically a part-time post. There would be physio sessions in the afternoon and then the training at night, when the players came in from their day jobs. There were three teams to look after, a first string and second string as well as the youth side. We were an amateur team in the best possible sense, with the players professional in so many ways despite the lack of a pay packet.

When I went in, I weighed up our strengths and weaknesses. Our players were part time, so I figured fitness might not be the strongest suit. I decided we would make sure we were faster and stronger than the rest. If we could take care of that, we'd win more games than we lost. I put them through it in training, but they responded well. We trained at Lesser Hampden but also did a lot of work in the big stadium, up and down those terraces. To a man, the players were absolutely fantastic.

I would without question argue that those were the happiest days of my football life. Not that I thought going through life happy was something to brag about – it was work after all – but I can't pretend I didn't enjoy it. I was fortunate to make some wonderful friends at Hampden, and those friendships have stood the test of time. People like Peter Buchanan, who played under me at that stage, are still great pals. I appreciated their efforts for me, and hopefully they could see I was totally committed to the job in hand.

The first season was very much a learning curve and we never really challenged for promotion, tailing off early into the campaign and ending up down in the 13th spot in what was a 19-team league at that point. When you consider Ayr United and Airdrie claimed the top two spots, you realise the size of clubs little old Queen's were up against.

It takes time to get your own ideas across and that first season was very much about doing that, together with implementing my own training methods and shaping things behind the scenes to suit the way I wanted things to run and the team to play.

As was always my goal, we improved year on year from that point on. In my second season, 1966–67, we edged up the table to finish seventh. Again, it was two big professional sides that went up, with Raith Rovers and Greenock Morton earning promotion.

The following year, we set off on a real adventure as we put together a serious promotion push. There was a great buzz around the club and around Glasgow, with so much affection for Queen's from all corners of the city. St Mirren were champions-elect from early on, but it was left for us to scrap with Arbroath and my old team East Fife for the second promotion place. What a fight it was, too. In the final shake-up, the table read St Mirren 62 points, Arbroath 52, East Fife 49, Queen's Park 48. Fourth place kept our progress steady, but we'd been within touching distance of Arbroath in second place, and it was a bitter blow when we pulled up short. Still, I was proud of the efforts of my players and their determination to buy into what I was trying to achieve.

At the business end of that season, we hit a fantastic streak of form, winning eight games on the bounce in a set of fixtures that included matches against our promotion rivals Arbroath and East Fife. Beating them both gave us a big boost, but ultimately it was not quite enough. We dropped three points in our last two games, losing at Stenhousemuir and drawing at home to Forfar, but we would have needed Arbroath to trip up in any case. They didn't oblige.

In fairness, we had a pleasant distraction that season as we won through to the quarter-finals of the League Cup – the first time the club had ever got to that stage in the competition. It was run in group stages at that time, before moving into the knockout phase, and we ended up going out at the hands of St Johnstone over two legs in the last eight.

We had some good fun in the cups around that time. In the 1966–67 season, we went on a decent run in the Scottish Cup after getting past Stenhousemuir, Raith Rovers and then, after a replay, Airdrie. Our reward? A wee trip across the city to play Celtic. This was, of course, the same Celtic side who were on their way to becoming European champions, and we had to go to their place with a team of amateurs who would be going into the game after a week of hard graft at their work. Again, there's nothing like a good old-fashioned challenge to get the adrenalin flowing.

Celtic had actually just played a European Cup tie on the

Wednesday of that week, when the Yugoslavian side Vojvodina Novi Sad had visited Glasgow. They hadn't got the warmest of welcomes. Jock Stein banned them from the usual training session on the pitch ahead of the game because, he claimed, of fears about the state of the surface. Cynics might suggest it also had a bit to do with the fact that his team had lost in the first leg over on the Continent, going down 1–0, and were desperate to do anything they could to turn things back in their advantage.

There was a place in the semi-final of the European Cup at stake, and Celtic were made to work for their victory, with a late goal from Billy McNeill giving them a 2–0 win on the night and putting them through 2–1 on aggregate. It had been a nervy affair and must have taken a lot out of them.

On top of that, the bad weather that Jock had been so concerned about had continued to sweep across Glasgow, and the torrential rain kept on coming. The pitch was going to be heavy, their legs were going to be tired. All in all, I thought to myself, 'We've got a chance here.' It was all stacking up in our favour.

Then a phone call came through to me. I was told there was doubt about the pitch at Celtic Park, that the game might not go ahead. I knew what was happening: Jock Stein was throwing his weight about to try to get the tie put off. Poor Queen's Park would have to toe the line. Another call came through, to say a referee was being sent to have a look at the park.

Big Jock then called: 'Pitch inspection at 10 a.m. on Saturday morning.' He was his usual brisk and bold self. I said, 'Fine, Jock, I'll be there.' So I turned up at 8.50 a.m. – and lo and behold, Jock was there along with the referee. Ten o'clock, my foot. When I walked onto the pitch, he looked like he'd seen a ghost. 'Hi, Jock, looks like I made it just in time,' I said.

So the inspection went ahead, and all the time Jock's in the background tutting, 'Terrible, terrible. There's no way we can play on this. It would be downright dangerous.'

I hit back, 'I thought the rules said that surface water was the deciding factor. It's soft, but there's no water lying.'

The referee was squirming by this point. He knew what he 'should' be doing, at least according to the big boys, but he also knew I was right. I made sure he heard me when I said, 'Wait until the press gets to hear about this.' Within seconds, he reached his verdict: 'The game's on.'

If Jock had been cursing me then, he would have been even more furious once the match kicked off and we gave them the fright of their lives. It was unthinkable for Queen's Park to go to Parkhead and win, but that's exactly what looked like happening for large chunks of the game.

We set out to put pressure on Celtic from the very first whistle, to hustle and harry at every opportunity. It worked. Tommy Gemmell got them off to the worst possible start when he scored an own goal inside the first minute, and the home crowd were nervous before they'd even settled into their places on the terracing.

Gemmell equalised with a penalty just seven minutes later, but we didn't capitulate. Niall Hopper, an important player for us up front, popped up with a couple of goals, and we had a real, real chance of the biggest upset the game had ever seen. It was nip and tuck, but Celtic's strength eventually saw them through, and they won 5–3 in what was one of the games of the season.

We had them really rattled, with Jimmy Johnstone sent off towards the end for retaliation. He ended up getting banned by the club for lashing out at Millar Hay. We had set out to show we wouldn't be intimidated, and the players followed my instructions to the letter, with a number of weighty but fair challenges during the course of the night to let Celtic know they were in a game.

But, Johnstone's rash act aside, it was played in the best possible spirit, and we gave a good account of ourselves. Still, with a win in the bag, it was Jock who could go home happiest . . . even if he was still beelin' about what had gone on earlier at the pitch inspection!

Maybe he was right, maybe it was dangerous, but I'd played in far worse myself. I can remember going up to Forfar with Rangers for a cup tie on one occasion and finding there was a particularly severe frost. We arrived half-expecting to be told the game was postponed, but to everyone's surprise it kicked off. It was then that we discovered there was a patch of ground, probably 40 yards by 10 yards, that was thick with ice. I was playing right-half and that piece of ground was just where I was playing in the first half.

People talk about Korea being dangerous – I tell you, give me a spell on the line any day of the week ahead of trying to play on that death trap of a pitch. I must have been flat on my back at least 20 times and was lucky not to have knocked myself out, or worse, when I hit the deck. I collared the referee and told him he had to call it off, but he said he'd get a lynching if he did. The show had to go on, and it did. If I'd had a pair of skates, it would have been far more use than the football boots I was skiting around on. Whenever we got possession, we made sure the ball was shifted to the 'good' side of the park, and in the second half I was at least spared that bit of ground.

That particular day, I also ended up challenging a member of the crowd, the first and last time I ever did that. I couldn't begin to repeat what this character was calling me every time the ball went out anywhere near where he was standing. In the end, I stopped, turned and pointed to him: 'You, you ... I'll see you outside at the final whistle. You and me.' The referee took umbrage. He said, 'Mr Davis, you cannot get involved like that.' The heckling stopped, though, and he never did meet me outside.

That's one thing you never got with a Queen's Park crowd. Our supporters were always good sports. The wonderful atmosphere that existed behind the scenes seemed to spread out onto the terraces, and it was always a joy to play in front of them, home and away.

On occasion, we ventured too far for even the most loyal of supporters to follow, not least on the far-flung tours we regularly conducted. Our many and varied connections around the world were behind our globetrotting ways – those and the spirit of adventure that the committee embraced.

One of our contacts was a tobacco company with links in Nigeria and Sierra Leone, and we travelled there in consecutive years to play local sides. The standard of football wasn't great in Africa at that point, not even equivalent to the Second Division at home, but the spirit of competition was strong and the experience was as good for us as it was for the host teams. Those tours did so much for the togetherness of the team, and we took that back with us and into our work when we were in more familiar surroundings.

We travelled to Nigeria on a couple of occasions, visiting two of the three districts in the country as they stood at that time. It was a fearsome place, with a real powderkeg atmosphere at every turn. It had been under British control until 1960, when it gained independence. The situation there was changing all the time, and the police were vicious, patrolling with guns and long batons and thinking nothing of beating anyone who didn't toe the line. We watched the country get more militarised, and it wasn't with great sadness that we didn't return.

When we ventured over in the summer of 1965, we played Eastern Nigeria, the Lagos Association and Northern Nigeria. It was a trek, with an overnight train taking us down to London to catch the flight out to Africa, but the more time we spent together the better, as far as I was concerned. I was just in the door as coach, and I knew I'd learn plenty about the men I was going to be working with while we were on the road.

They weren't the easiest of circumstances to play in, either, given the tensions in Africa, so that helped pull us together and give us a common bond. It was a great introduction to the job and only served to reinforce what I already knew about the characters in the group and the spirit they had.

With my Queen's team, I also went Down Under, playing at Canberra on the east coast of Australia and in New Zealand on the North Island. Again, those were wonderful experiences for manager and players alike. The football was good and we didn't lose too many matches. It was a chance to express ourselves and go out and enjoy the games away from the competitive action back home.

In saying that, the expectations at Queen's Park were very realistic, and that helped to foster the type of freedom we were trying to instil in the players. For me, it was a whole new way of life. I think when you spent time in the Old Firm, on either side, you become accustomed to living with a certain amount of pressure on your shoulders. It is unlike playing for or coaching any other team, in that you are expected by everyone – supporters, media, management and directors – to win every game you play, and that includes Old Firm derbies themselves.

When you spend several years in that type of environment – in my case, eight years – your mindset changes to fit with those peculiar demands. Then, when you move on and you find yourself in a far less pressurised situation, it's like starting all over again. It's a totally different game, not necessarily better or worse, and because of that you get fresh wind in your sails. That certainly happened for me at Queen's, with the added factor that it was my first job as a manager in my own right. I was determined to do things right, and I think I proved myself well.

I was very conscious that the relationship between me and the squad had to be balanced. I didn't want to be a dictator whom they were scared of, but I had to command the respect that every coach needs. I'd do what I could to lighten the mood when the time was right. I had a routine of going round the dressing-room before the game and addressing each of the players one by one with specific instructions. I'd go round every one of them, then when I came to Malky Mackay I'd give it: 'Malky ... you just, well, you ...' The boys would wait for it and they knew exactly what I meant – Malky was a great character and a great player, but he was a law unto himself.

The club had been a good breeding ground for young players; even the most unconventional had a chance to shine with the Spiders. Just a few years before I arrived, a certain Alex Ferguson had made his breakthrough, the most famous FP of all. The young Fergie was a bustling striker with a nose for goal and a heart as big as a lion's, the type of attitude that took him to where he is today. There's a lesson in there for every youngster: if you try hard enough, and keep trying, you can be whatever you want to be. Nobody at Hampden could possibly have predicted where Sir Alex, as we should call him now, would end up, but he had it within him to drive himself forward and grab every opportunity that came his way.

There was a steady stream of good prospects coming through the ranks. During my time, we had players in the youth ranks of the calibre of Andy Lynch, who went on to star for Hearts and Celtic. I worked with Andy from when he first joined us, at the age of around 12. It was always pleasing to see a boy go on and make something of himself in the game as he did.

The youth team was more important to Queen's than to any other team, because it was a way of ensuring we had a supply of players available for the main side, all of whom had been schooled in our way of thinking and given the best start in the game by virtue of good early coaching. After all, we couldn't just go out and buy somebody from one of our rivals to plug a gap.

Aside from the youngsters, though, we had our pick of the best of the amateur leagues and would regularly invite players along to big open trial sessions, where we'd put them through their paces and pick out the ones with a chance of making it as a senior. There was never any shortage of volunteers, despite no prospect of pay. After all, which player wouldn't want the chance to call Hampden their home?

A big part in our success was down to our willingness to use a substitute in most games. Up to that stage, teams resisted putting on their extra man unless injury meant it was a necessity. I decided it would be to our advantage to make use of the resources we had at hand, especially given our amateur status. We had players who were still finding their feet in the senior game; if they began to tire, I was happy to whip them off and put on a fresh pair of legs. We had a couple of players, Brian Mulgrew and Willie McLanachan, who were perfectly suited to the role of 'super-sub'. Mulgrew's great strength was his pace, while McLanachan had a cannonball of a shot that made him very useful if we were chasing a game.

We had players in the first team who had a great chance of progressing, and Millar Hay was another superb prospect. I felt sure he would go on and make his name as a professional, and Millar served Clyde and Hamilton Accies with distinction.

All of those names and more bring the stories flooding back for me, and I'm proud to have been part of the fantastic Queen's Park story, a history like no other in Scottish football. I still keep in touch with the club and attend quite a few functions, always getting the best of treatment and having great fun. All of the supporters are like one big family, and I've got great memories. It was a different atmosphere from being at a club the size of Rangers, and a nice one to be involved in. I have nothing but fond memories of that period in my life.

My reputation in management circles was certainly growing. I was asked to coach Scotland's amateur international team, taking the squad to Spain for the European Nations Cup. Perhaps I was biased, but I ended up with fourteen Queen's Park players in the squad, along with one from Partick Thistle and another from Glasgow University.

I was also involved with the Scottish national team, working with the manager Bobby Brown as one of his coaches for the preparations for the 1970 World Cup qualifiers. Bobby's plan was to call upon a batch of different trainers, and when I was invited along it was with Tom McNiven of Hibs and John Cumming of Hearts. That was at the end of the summer of 1968, while I was still at Queen's, so I didn't have far to walk from my office for the Scotland squad session.

At one stage, I was even touted as a future Scotland manager in my own right. It was towards the end of 1966, not too long after I'd started off coaching with Queen's. They were looking for someone to take over after Ian McColl and John Prentice had departed in relatively quick succession, and the *Evening Times* ran a hit list of six young coaches with potential for the top job. In at number one was Harold Davis, followed, in order, by none other than Davie White, who was still at Clyde at that point, Airdrie's Archie Wright, Walter McCrae at Kilmarnock, Third Lanark's Francis Joyner and Ally MacLeod of Ayr United. At least Ally proved the reporter right by eventually going on to get his shot at the Scotland job.

It wasn't something I'd ever seriously contemplated, however flattering it might be to see your name up in lights. My focus was on Queen's and on continuing the progress we were already making. But, as anyone will tell you, it's very difficult to chart a smooth course in football management. Just when I was really hitting my stride, Rangers came looming back on the horizon, and my life was about to be thrown upside down.

It was in the autumn of 1969 that the approach came from Davie White at Ibrox. He wanted me to join his coaching staff and asked me to give it serious consideration. While it had been easy to pledge myself to Queen's more than four years earlier, this wasn't a decision I took lightly.

Davie had come in to take over from Scot Symon during the 1967–68 season, so it would have been unfair to judge him on the results that term. He'd had the 1968–69 season to himself, to put across his own ideas, but the results had been indifferent. Celtic had, again, won the league, and they'd also beaten Davie's team 4–0 in the Scottish Cup final to rub salt into already raw wounds. The start of the 1969–70 season hadn't been flawless either, and, in the weeks leading up to the approach to Queen's for my services, consecutive defeats against Ayr United and Celtic had put Stein's side on the front foot very early in proceedings.

Did I want to get myself mixed up in what was clearly a very difficult situation developing at Rangers? Should I give up being my own man to take on a coaching role under another manager? What would the impact be on Queen's Park if I upped and left just a few months into the season? All of those questions were swimming around my head after the call came from Davie.

But, at the end of the day, it was Rangers Football Club, and there was only one decision I could come to: it was time to go home.

I had some great years at Hampden, and they were devastated when I left, but to their credit nobody begrudged me the opportunity to go back to Ibrox. They all understood the pull that the club had, and I left with the best wishes of everyone ringing in my ears.

22

FEELING BLUE

WHEN I LEFT RANGERS AS a player, I hoped one day I would be back. I didn't know when or in what capacity, but I had a feeling that I wasn't quite finished at Ibrox just yet, and so it proved to be. When it happened for me, it was with excitement and a hint of trepidation that I walked back through the door. I was on the other side of the fence now, not one of the lads but one of the management team.

It was on Monday, 29 September 1969 that my return was announced. It had been brewing for a while by then; I'd had a lot to consider before I'd eventually decided to agree to it. I was settled at Hampden and had no burning desire to leave Queen's Park, where I was building for the future and felt we had an excellent bunch of players with a good chance of success in the years ahead.

But it was Rangers Football Club, the team that had got under my skin during my playing days at Ibrox. As much as my head told me it made sense to stay and be my own man with Queen's, my heart was crying out for me to go back. And I followed my heart.

I'd spent four years as a manager in my own right at a club where I was allowed to be my own boss, without any interference, but I was comfortable with the idea of relinquishing that control and falling in line under Davie White. Although I didn't know him well when he first approached me to join him, I had spoken to him at length about what he wanted from me and his plans for the team, and I liked what I heard. Many of his ideas went hand in glove with my own thoughts on the game, so I couldn't foresee any reason why I wouldn't be able to work well with him.

I may have played against him when he was at Clyde as a wing-half in the 1950s and '60s, but I don't recall it if I did. That was about as far as our connection went: we had played at roughly the same time as each other. That, as much as anything, was why I was surprised, pleasantly so, to get his invitation.

The first contact had actually been a couple of years previously, when Davie was put in charge at Rangers. He spoke to me and sounded me out about the possibility of joining his staff, and I was keen to find out more. It all fell to pieces when he discovered he couldn't get the money to recruit the extra body he wanted, so I was left to get on with my job at Hampden. I do wonder from time to time what might have been if we'd been paired together from the start, if we'd had a proper run at it. I'm sure it would have worked out differently, but I never got that chance.

When he came back for a second bite, it wasn't totally unexpected, but I wasn't waiting by the phone, either. For one thing, I couldn't see why the money would suddenly be found to pay the extra salary if the directors hadn't been keen in the first place. I was happy to get on with my work at Queen's and go on the basis of 'what will be will be'. In time, I got the nod to speak to Davie again, and things snowballed from there. I was on my way back to Ibrox.

My eventual appointment was part of a major overhaul of Davie's staff. He had basically decided that he was light on coaching staff, with the first-team duties falling pretty much solely on Davie Kinnear's shoulders. Under the reshuffle, Davie

Kinnear reverted to his role as physiotherapist, taking care of injuries and treatment, swapping places with Lawrie Smith, who had been working as physio but now stepped up to take on the role of chief coach. Lawrie had followed the manager when he had moved from Clyde, so clearly they had a good understanding and working relationship.

I was recruited as assistant coach, with Lawrie and I sharing duties on the training ground with the manager, who wanted to get even more hands-on than he was already. Having been frustrated by the lack of progress up to that point, he felt the three of us working together could get the job done and implement the ideas he had for the team.

My old Partick Thistle boss Willie Thornton retained his place as assistant manager. He was a real father figure for everyone at the club, and one of football's true gentlemen. Willie had been taken back to Ibrox from Firhill when Davie had first been appointed, perhaps with the board conscious of the new manager's relative youth. They clearly thought that putting a Rangers man like Willie alongside Davie would add weight to the new management team. Willie had managed Dundee prior to spending a long stint with Thistle, and part of his new Rangers remit was scouting. He was assigned to lend an extra pair of eyes when it came to identifying the manager's signing targets.

With my addition and the promotion of Lawrie Smith, there was a strong, expanded backroom team in place. I think that hinted at the size of the task Davie felt he had at Ibrox, and his understanding that he couldn't do it all on his own. It had taken him time to get the coaching staff in place. I don't know if he'd realised when he was first appointed exactly what was required. I do know it had taken time to persuade the powers that be to invest in more backroom staff.

I relished the opportunity to return to Ibrox, excited by the way the manager had sold the job to me and by his plans for the future. It wasn't a case of coming in and taking over from someone else or slotting into a traditional role; it was part of a complete revamp of the way things were done at the club.

Training schedules were revised, and Davie continued with his policy of refusing to split the squad into first team and second team for training purposes. Everyone worked together on the training field, doing the same things and learning the same lessons. It was a bid to get everyone singing from the same hymn sheet.

When I walked into the dressing-room for the first time as coach, I was far from a stranger. There were plenty of familiar faces, people I'd played alongside who were still on the books, as well as some of the young boys who had been at Ibrox back then who were now establishing themselves in the first team.

Boys like John Greig, Ronnie McKinnon, Willie Henderson and Jim Baxter had been my teammates, but I didn't feel uncomfortable in my new role. I suppose I'd always been a bit of an authority figure anyway, even during my playing days, so it wasn't as if I had to change completely. I'd been the one they would come to with questions or problems; they called me 'the Professor' because of it. If anyone had anything to find out, the call was always, 'Ask Harry.'

So going back as a coach wasn't daunting, and I felt I knew how to handle the senior players well. In addition to my role on the training side, I was handed responsibility for the reserve team and would take them home and away, so my skills in dealing with the younger members of the staff also came under scrutiny. The reserves were a formidable unit, a match for most of the first teams outside of the Old Firm, I would say, and I could hold my head up high as far as my record was concerned in matches.

The work with the first-team players during the week was, of course, just as important in the grand scheme of things. When I arrived, the biggest problem appeared to be a lack of confidence, spreading right through the team from the front to the back. There had been a lot of flak flying in the direction of the players and the manager, much of it orchestrated by a certain Willie Waddell in his role as a football writer and authoritative figure in the game due to his experience and his Rangers past.

He had famously tagged the manager 'the Boy David' as part of what seemed like a campaign to undermine Davie at every turn. It must have had an impact on the manager, even if he never let it show. He was a pragmatic character, a draughtsman by trade, who would not have needed football to give him a decent living. He could have walked away at any point, turned his back on the game and gone on with his life in his former profession without any worries. Maybe that helped him put things in perspective and not get too wrapped up in what was being said about him. He always chose to ignore criticism, preferring instead to get on with the things he could change, by working with the team and striving for improvement.

Despite the negative attention from the press, or at least certain quarters of it, there was no defeatist attitude. Davie White knew what he wanted to do and was pushing ahead with those plans. By rejigging the coaching staff, he hoped to give a fresh feel to things, a new impetus to the season.

Undoubtedly, he would have loved to have strengthened his hand on the playing side too, but by that stage the purse strings had tightened. Perhaps the directors were already getting edgy about what path they would take in the future and weren't keen to splash the cash in the way they had when he'd been backed to sign Colin Stein and Alex MacDonald. Even with hefty outlays on those types of players to begin with, Rangers were still turning a handsome profit when Davie was at the helm, and that side of the job shouldn't be underestimated. He was running a tight ship and sticking to the budget set out by the directors.

Nobody would argue that Stein and MacDonald did not prove

to be worth their weight in gold to Rangers over their time at the club, so there was no question that the manager had wasted any of the funds he had been given to invest. It's just unfortunate that the funds appeared to dry up as his reign came to an end, because he clearly had an eye for a player and knew the type he needed to make his plans fall into place.

While Davie didn't have the sort of playing background that I or many of the others who were around Ibrox at that time had, his coaching credentials were decent. He had been chosen by Clyde to replace John Prentice when he had been snapped up by the SFA to take over the Scotland team in 1966. At Shawfield, he took Clyde up as high as third in the First Division, an excellent achievement with a club that was not expected to do great things.

The thing about Davie was that he was learning all the time, even after he got the big job at Rangers. As manager at Clyde, he had been almost obsessive about learning the trade of coaching, following Celtic on their European Cup run in 1966–67 and Rangers on their adventure in the European Cup-Winners' Cup in the same year. His attention to detail, in watching both halves of the Old Firm going about their work in training, caught Scot Symon's eye, and he invited Davie to become his assistant at Rangers. It was a rapid rise, but understandably he accepted the offer. Within a few weeks, though, Symon had become the first manager ever to be sacked by Rangers. I think the directors had hoped that he would remain in place and take on an overseeing role, as general manager, but he rejected that out of hand. I can understand why he chose to make a clean break; it must have been a very painful end to a wonderful coaching career. Symon's achievements with Rangers will forever be among the greatest of any manager. The Boss will always be an important figure in the history of the club.

He was a veteran when he stepped aside, and his replacement was the polar opposite, a young man with very little experience.

There were a lot of differences between the two. Symon was very much a figurehead who took a step back from the day-to-day running of the team, while Davie liked to get his hands dirty, get out on the training pitch with his tracksuit on and be in the middle of everything.

In his first season, he could have become a hero. All he needed was a win at home to Aberdeen to clinch the league. But the Dons won 3–2, Celtic took the title and the chance was gone. After that, he whisked his team away to Scandinavia for three weeks of intensive training, working heavily on set pieces and organisation during the summer tour of 1968. He wanted to play a more attacking and free-flowing type of system than had been seen at the club previously, and he shuffled personnel around to fit, causing a bit of a stir by moving Willie Johnston inside from his place on the wing to feature centrally and shifting Sandy Jardine forward from defence into midfield.

It was a move to a 4–3–3 formation in essence, and there were murmurs of discontent about that from various quarters. It was progress, but some people simply don't like to see change. Had Davie's reshaped team gone out and won everything in sight, I'm sure those people would have changed their minds. As it happened, it didn't quite work out that way. In the 1968–69 season, Celtic ran away with the league and Davie's side were well beaten in the Scottish Cup.

It was against that backdrop that I was taken to the club, early in the 1969 season, when the wagons were circling and the critics appeared to be lining up to take a pop. That could have put me off joining in the first place, but, if anything, it made me more determined to make a go of things and prove the doubters wrong.

By the time I arrived, 13 games of the season had passed. It did, eventually, prove to be unlucky for me. As was traditional at that point, the League Cup group games had raised the curtain and served as the warm-up before the First Division action began.

Those matches had not gone to plan, although an unfortunate draw did not help. Celtic landed up in the same group as Rangers. They beat Airdrie home and away in the pool and also won the home tie against Celtic. A 1–0 defeat at Parkhead in the next game redressed the balance, though, and in the end Rangers failed to qualify for the quarter-finals of the competition by virtue of drawing 3–3 with Raith Rovers at Ibrox. It was the type of little slip that can be the difference between success and failure for the Old Firm teams.

In the league, they had won seven points from a possible twelve by the time I checked in. Draws against Dundee and defeats against Ayr and Celtic made it tough going, although a 2–0 win against Steaua Bucharest in the first round of the European Cup-Winners' Cup had given reason to be optimistic.

The first game after I returned to Ibrox was the second leg of that European tie, a trip to Romania and a potential banana skin if ever there was one. We came through it, drawing 0–0 to move forward in the competition and keep spirits high.

The league form continued to be decent, and Celtic's initial confidence was being dented. There were a couple of blips in the autumn, with a defeat at home to a very decent Hibs side and a draw at Motherwell, but they were by no means catastrophic for our title hopes. There was a belief that we could do it, that Celtic's dominance could be ended.

In Europe, too, there was a determination to prove we were heading in the right direction, but Górnik Zabrze had something to say about that. The Poles beat us 3–1 at their ground and came to Ibrox on 26 November 1969 hoping to finish the job. That proved to be a black day for Davie and, ultimately, me and the bulk of his coaching staff. A matching 3–1 defeat in a dismal game at Ibrox ensured our exit from Europe for the season.

It was also the end of the manager's tenure. The crowd, paying heed to everything that was being said and written by the media, had started to turn, and unfortunately there was no way back. There was a board meeting at the ground on the night of the Górnik game and apparently the decision was unanimous: Davie was to be dismissed. It wasn't until he turned up for work the next day that he found out he was out of a job.

As usual, there was a flurry of speculation about who would take over. The *Evening Times* on the day of the announcement of the sacking made interesting reading. Brian Clough, who was out of work after quitting Derby County, was one of the names mentioned, while his Derby player Dave Mackay was another said to be interested. Closer to home, the *Times* suggested in the same article that George Farm at Dunfermline was a contender and also said that I would be in the running for the job, given my place on the staff and my history with the club. Willie Thornton, who was appointed caretaker manager, was another Rangers name linked with the job.

But I don't think any of us on the inside were fooled by what was being written. From where we stood, it looked as though Willie Waddell had worked his ticket perfectly; he'd engineered the downfall of Davie and was perfectly placed to take his job. That was exactly the way it all panned out, just as so many of us had expected it would.

There were a lot of kind words spoken about the departing manager by the players, with people like John Greig jumping to his defence. John described him as a 'friend to everyone' when he was interviewed at the time, and perhaps it was beginning to sink in that they had lost exactly that: a good friend, a man who would fight their corner. They wouldn't get the same when the next manager was appointed. Willie Henderson was another who spoke in support of Davie, and so too did Jim Baxter. I've made my feelings on Jim known, but the manager had chosen to give him a second chance and take him back to Ibrox. Unfortunately, his work ethic hadn't changed.

It was all well and good coming out with platitudes in the press after the event. The disappointing thing was that more wasn't done while Davie was still in place to make sure the sacking didn't happen in the first place. Ultimately, it is players who cost managers their jobs. Certainly that was the case in this instance, because he was busting a gut to do things the right way. The response was not always what it should have been in terms of application in training, at least not from what I saw in the short time I was on the staff. Davie was only the twelfth man ever to occupy the manager's office, but he had become the second to be sacked, hard on the heels of Scot Symon. All was not well, and clearly the directors were impatient for a return to the type of success they had been accustomed to.

It was in December 1969 that Waddell's appointment was confirmed, and in the first instance there was no change to the backroom team. There was no indication of the long-term plans in that regard, but I wasn't comfortable. I just couldn't envisage myself working with him for any substantial period of time. Something would have had to give at some point, and I'm not one to back down.

I never took to him at all. For one thing, every second word was an expletive. His language was absolutely vile, even in front of women. I think he thought it made him look tough, but that never cut it with me. He came in effing and blinding from the start, trying to lay down the law to the players before he'd seen them kick a ball. He ordered double training sessions right away and made great play of the fact that discipline was going to be his major focus. That was a bit of a smokescreen, since the fitness and discipline were already at a high standard, but Waddell knew how to play the media; he was spinning the message exactly the way he wanted it to be spun.

Still, I was prepared to bide my time and see how things shaped up. At one stage, when he was still sizing people up and watching over the training sessions, Waddell took me upstairs. I thought I was getting the heave right away, but instead he told me he liked my style. He told me he'd seen the way I worked with the young players and the senior team and appreciated the way I changed my style to suit each group. Apparently, that didn't count for an awful lot in the long run. He stabbed me in the back not too long after that pep talk, sacking me along with the rest of the staff he had inherited.

It was on 17 April 1970 that my departure was announced in the press. Lawrie Smith and Davie Kinnear were fired on the same day, a sad one for the three of us, who had busted a gut to do our best for the club and were rewarded with our P45s. It was tough to take, but that's the nature of the beast of football.

He was washing out any remnants of Davie White's tenure, and getting rid of us was part of the process. Jock Wallace was taken in from Hearts to become his right-hand man. Just like Davie's before, Waddell's backroom team was taking shape. Stan Anderson was the other man handed a place on his team, as trainer, recruited from Clyde along with the physio Tom Craig. It was all change again.

Wallace was the key appointment, having served as assistant manager at Hearts for less than two years when he was lured across to Glasgow. Prior to that, he'd been player-manager at Berwick Rangers, but it was his experience of the Army and the training methods he had taken from his service that gained him the most attention. It seemed to me there was a certain amount of irony in bringing in one old soldier to replace another, but there wasn't an awful lot of logic being used at that time.

The most galling thing was that the team had been playing well before Waddell had arrived, save for some uncharacteristic results here and there, and we thought we were making good progress. In fact, we knew we were. It takes time to put your own stamp on things and get your own ideas across, and unfortunately Davie wasn't given that time. Neither were the rest of us.

To say I never regarded Waddell highly would be an understatement. There's a right way of treating people, and sadly he didn't have it. Davie Kinnear, Lawrie Smith and I were called up one by one to be told the bad news just a week before the end of the season. Between then and when he had taken over, Waddell had contrived to turn a winnable position in the league into a resounding defeat. Celtic won at a canter, with a twelve-point advantage, and in the last ten games of the season the team won just twice and lost five games. It was a horrendous run of form under the guidance of the new manager, and it felt like we were being made scapegoats. He hadn't made an impact in the Scottish Cup, either, with Celtic beating us in the quarter-finals.

If the directors had been hoping for a quick lift following the media clamour to have Davie White ousted, they had miscalculated in a massive way. Form took a dive, and we were fortunate to finish second, with Hibs moving within a point of us by the time the last game had been played.

It must have been an eye-opener for Waddell himself. Obviously, he was already steeped in the traditions of the club, having been a player, but until you've been involved at first hand in preparing a Rangers team for a game it is difficult to comprehend what's required. It is easy to criticise when you're sitting in a comfortable seat in the press-box, far more difficult to turn things around in a practical way. He had to get to know the players and discover whether they had the tools to fit into the system he wanted to play. There was no quick fix.

He evidently thought that clearing the decks was the way forward, and his wish was granted. I left Rangers for the second time in my career. The difference this time was that I wasn't so confident I'd be back. It was desperately disappointing, but I dusted myself down and got on with my life.

Waddell did the same, and I'm sure he didn't give me a second thought, at least not until we were briefly reunited three years later when I was back at a centenary event at Edmiston House. It was the first time I'd been back for a Rangers function, and I was happy to be there. I wasn't bitter towards the club; there was no way I would have spited myself or disrespected Rangers by refusing to attend.

There was a big crowd in, with all of the players and ex-players invited to attend the celebrations. I was settling down at my table when I noticed one of the young players sidling up. It was Alex Willoughby, whom I'd had under my wing when I was coaching at Ibrox. I had an awful lot of time for Alex. He was a cracking prospect and a lovely lad into the bargain. I had left behind many friends at Ibrox when I'd been moved on, and this was a great opportunity to meet up again and catch up with them, just like the good old days.

Alex said to me, 'Harry, I've got a message: the manager would like a word with you.'

I put him straight on that score. I said, 'Tell him to go f**k himself.'

I've no idea what Alex actually relayed to Waddell, or whether he was quite as forceful as I would have liked, but he dutifully went back across the room and passed on some version of my response. Within a minute, he was back at my table: 'The manager's really upset. Please go and have a word with him.'

Well, like the big softie I really am, I went across. He was stiff as you like, but Waddell said, 'I'd like to apologise. I should never have sacked you. I'm deeply sorry.'

I replied, 'Is that it?' I turned on my heel and walked away back to the other side of the room. That was the last time I ever spoke to him.

Prior to his arrival, I'd been taking the reserves and also first-team training sessions. I carried on in that vein after Waddell had been appointed, and the results continued to be impressive. The young team didn't lose a game while I was in charge.

One of the problems we had was that every single move was being watched. One of the others on the training staff was up and down the stairs to the manager's office telling him everything that was said and done. We all got the sack – apart from him. Surprise, surprise.

So that was it, the dream return was over. I had swithered about going back to Ibrox, and pretty quickly I discovered that it hadn't been the right decision. But then, if I had turned down the opportunity and it had not arisen again in the future, I would have gone through life wondering, 'What if?' I gave it a go, I did my best and unfortunately that wasn't good enough for the man at the top.

23

BACK TO WORK

IF THERE IS A POSITIVE to leaving a club like Rangers, it is surely that you rarely struggle to find other opportunities. Just as I'd found when it came to being freed as a player, the fact I'd been at Ibrox gave me credentials that were attractive to other clubs.

Pretty soon afterwards, I was given the opportunity to get back on the bike again and take up the manager's position at Queen of the South. I accepted, although in hindsight I probably shouldn't have. My heart wasn't in it the way it had been with Queen's Park, and I spent just a year at Palmerston Park.

The role was as manager and coach, a joint title that would, I thought, give me complete control of all the playing matters and let me be my own man again. It was a part-time job, and, with the family settled in Glasgow, it made sense not to uproot us all to Dumfries. Instead, I shuttled back and forth up that long road for training and home games. It was a big commitment, but one that I felt was worth making to get back in the game.

I left Rangers at the end of April 1970 and by June that year I was heading through the front door at Palmerston to take up my new position. In my own playing days, Queen of the South had been a decent force in the First Division, but they had drifted out of the top league around the time I'd left Rangers as a player and had been out of it in the years that had passed since then. They had come close to returning on a few occasions, and in the season before I'd been taken on they had just missed out to Falkirk and Cowdenbeath. It suggested there was a decent squad to work with there and that the club had scope to grow and progress.

Unlike at Queen's Park, I'd be operating in the professional ranks, so I'd have a different pool of players to pick from and could go out and pay wages to attract the ones I wanted. There wasn't a huge budget by any means, but we were on a level footing with most of the other clubs in the Second Division.

My intention was to follow the blueprint I'd used at Hampden and concentrate on getting everyone fighting fit and ready to compete before building the team the way I wanted it to be built. That was the theory, at least. The practice turned out to be very different, and the reason was a certain Billy Houliston. He was the man who had recruited me, the chairman of the club.

But Billy, more importantly, was a playing legend at Queen of the South. He was the only man the club has ever had who won a full Scottish international cap, and he will forever be among their greats. He was a big, powerful centre-forward who scored a lot of goals in the Dumfries team's colours on his way to three appearances for the national side.

He was Dumfries born and bred, and started playing for his local club after serving in the RAF in the Second World War. Before long, he'd won the nickname 'Basher' because of his fearless approach to the game, and he became an idol, even more so once he'd made his Scotland debut in 1948. He played with Queen of the South until 1952, moving to Berwick Rangers and Third Lanark for short spells before packing it in.

Our swords never crossed on the pitch – he was winding down just as I was starting out with Rangers – so my first involvement with him was in his capacity as a director, when he asked me to accept the position of manager. He'd been on the board since

1957, so he was well and truly in with the bricks. He was Mr Queen of the South and a big figure around the town. We met, we discussed the move and everything seemed to be perfect.

What I should have done was have a closer look at the name of my predecessor on the list of managers. It wasn't Bobby Shearer, who had spent time in charge at Palmerston when I was at Queen's Park, nor was it Jackie Husband, who had followed Bobby into the hot seat. No, the name was a Mr Board of Directors. For two seasons in between Jackie leaving and my appointment, the board, led by Billy Houliston, had been running the team. They had done the same before appointing Bobby Shearer, who'd arrived a year after George Farm had departed for pastures new.

I knew the situation, of course, but I didn't appreciate what it meant for me as the new manager. I had presumed that, because they had gone to the trouble of giving me the job, they would want me to do it. What I discovered was that Billy was very much in charge at Palmertson. He ran the club from top to bottom, and that included picking the team. It would have been better to have been aware of that before I joined, but once I'd checked in I quickly found that it wasn't going to be easy.

Billy's son Keith was on the books as a player, and that brought its own problems for me. I coached him, tried to pass on a little of my experience, but it always seemed to me as though he was getting different advice from his father and that there would be only one winner when it came to who he'd listen to most.

All I could do was try to make the best of the situation, although from very early on I knew it wasn't really for me. For one thing, the commuting to Dumfries wasn't ideal. On paper, it was fine, but once I'd started driving up and down I quickly came to the conclusion that it wasn't a long-term proposition. But the main issue was the lack of overall control I had. I told myself I'd give it a season, see it through to the end, and that was what I did.

Results were average. We finished a point outside the top ten but well short of a promotion challenge.

Early in the season, we had been up there challenging to push our way into the top two or three, but it faded away as time went on, and we settled down behind the chasing pack. Naturally, the Scottish Cup brought me back into contact with Celtic; it seemed my destiny to be drawn to play Jock Stein's team wherever I went. It didn't go as well as our contest with them at Queen's Park had, and we ended up going down 5–1 at Parkhead in the third round. Still, it would have brought in a few pounds in gate receipts, at least.

If I'd been given my own head of steam, I might have been able to do more over the course of that season and beyond, but we'll never know. Even in the best of circumstances, a season is never long enough to get things the way you'd like them to be. I don't really judge myself on how things worked out because it wasn't a 'normal' managerial job, if there ever was such a thing.

I also don't beat myself up too much about only staying for a season. They might as well have fitted a revolving door, there were that many managers and coaches coming in and out during that period. Very few lasted more than a year, as Bobby Shearer and Jackie Husband could testify. The geography probably didn't help, either, and I think Bobby had similar problems to mine with the idea of committing to a club so far removed from our roots in the Central Belt.

Jim Easton, who followed me, lasted a couple of years, and so too did Willie McLean, but that was about as good as it got in terms of a shelf life at the Doonhamers. There was a succession of men before and after me who must all have faced similar challenges.

It was another one to put down to experience, but I came away from it quite content, really. Billy Houliston had his way of doing things and that was his prerogative; he was in charge and you couldn't argue about the fact that he loved the club. He lived and breathed Queen of the South, and maybe at times he just cared too much to be able to let go and let anyone else have a great deal of input. He wouldn't have been the first and certainly wasn't the last chairman to expect to have a say on team matters. Just look at Hearts and Vladimir Romanov and you'll see it's still going on today. Some managers are willing to live with it; I wasn't.

I left in the summer of 1971, and it took another four years for them to finally get the promotion back to the First Division that everyone at the club craved. It was Willie McLean who won it for them, taking them up as runners-up to Falkirk by a single point. Mind you, they just made it: Montrose finished level with them but were nudged back to third place on goal difference.

24

A HAPPY REUNION

AFTER THE DISAPPOINTMENT OF LEAVING Rangers, I have to admit I fell out of love with football. I was sickened by the way we had been treated, not least because just a few months earlier I'd given up a job I absolutely loved at Queen's Park to move across the city to Ibrox again. I was repaid with the sack not long after – a lovely reward.

I'd had my year at Queen of the South and could have started looking for another job in management after that. There were certainly opportunities out there as the merry-go-round continued to spin. But I decided I'd had enough, so I chose to get right away from it all.

Vi and I moved to Fife to take on the smallholding that my mother had passed on to me. It was a poultry operation, and it built up into a good business, producing eggs that were being delivered far and wide. It was tough going, but neither of us has ever been afraid of hard work, and we threw ourselves into it.

Then football came looming large on the horizon again. Davie White had been hurt as much as me by the Rangers experience, but he had been tempted back into the manager's seat by Dundee FC. It was early in December 1971 that the announcement was made: 'White Back in Business' was the headline. He'd been out of the game for two years but was obviously still held in high regard in the Dens boardroom, and it was a chance he was excited about, not least because he was taking over a team that was doing pretty nicely. Having finished fifth in the First Division the previous season, they were on course for the same placing in the 1971–72 campaign during which he came into the club.

He could see the potential at Dens Park. They'd been one of the biggest in the land not that long before and the task was to re-establish the team as genuine challengers to the Old Firm and the likes of Aberdeen. There wasn't a huge pot of gold for him to dip into and bring in big-name players, but he wasn't the type of manager who necessarily needed that. He was able to work with what he had and get them organised and capable of beating anyone on their day – as we went on to prove.

At around the time he was negotiating to take over at Dundee, Davie was plaguing me to go there with him. Initially, I'd been reluctant. At the back of my mind was the thought of what we'd experienced together at Ibrox: did I really want to put myself through that again? But Davie could be a persuasive man when he needed to be, and eventually I caved in. I said I'd give it a go, starting work in January 1972 when Davie himself took up the reins.

His appointment, as successor to John Prentice, had been announced a month earlier, but he was given time to get his business commitments in order before starting work. He'd been running a pub with Willie Henderson after leaving the Rangers job, so there were loose ends to tie up.

John, who had been Scotland manager prior to taking charge at Dundee, had planned to leave at the end of the season, but his departure was speeded up when rumours of his intention to step down began to circulate early. He'd been a bit frustrated by the lack of funds and by some of the attendance figures, which weren't always great despite the fact that his side was doing well, but those weren't factors that worried Davie or me overly much.

As far as my own work commitments were concerned, I had to dig deep and come up with all my own powers of persuasion to convince Vi to do the hard graft at the farm while I went back to football. She did a sterling job running the farm. I still did my bit with the deliveries in the morning, running around like a mad thing in our big old truck, dropping off batches of eggs in towns and villages all over the area. Eventually, we had to get a member of staff onboard to help us out; it was becoming impossible to do it all.

I'd told Davie I'd give it my all at Dundee, and that was what I did. It went so sweetly. The pair of us got on great, and I really enjoyed working with him. The reason he had been so heavily criticised at Ibrox was because he wasn't a Rangers player; he didn't have the stature in the game of a John Greig or an Ally McCoist to earn him a honeymoon period. He also didn't have the physical stature, either – he stands 5 ft 8 in. and is as lean as a whippet, so he wasn't a hulk of a man who could rule a dressing-room with an iron fist. But then again, he had me for that.

What he lacked in muscle, Davie made up for in ideas. If you took the time to listen to him when he was in full flow, he spoke so much sense and saw things that other people didn't. The problem was that too many players wouldn't take the time to listen; they weren't prepared to give him the benefit of the doubt. When Davie started going into detail, you could see some of the boys starting to drift off. They were in that dressing-room in body but not in mind. That's why we were a good combination. I was there to kick arse if people started to let their attention wander.

He had so many things he wanted to implement. For the first time in my career, I was learning about crossing over of strikers, working on pulling other teams out of position. That was just one of his theories. There were many, many more. He had his own ideas on the defensive aspects of the game, but understandably he gave me my head with that, and I was able to do a lot of work on the organisational side of what we did. We worked well together on the training field, and he let me have a decent input into the way things were done and the way we played.

I thoroughly enjoyed it, come rain, hail or shine. If the weather was bad, we'd head for the beach and do our work down there. I just loved being out on the training pitch, or sands.

We had a great bunch of guys – in the main, at least. I fell out with a couple of them, including Gordon Strachan. He was just a young boy starting out then, but he had a big-time attitude. I'd say to him, 'Why do you never pass the ball?' He said that was a load of rubbish, but it wasn't – he was playing for himself and would run it until he lost it. He played his own way back then. I got the feeling that his father was effectively his coach and that nobody else's opinion counted. Mind you, a certain Sir Alex managed to get the best out of him at Aberdeen, and the rest, as they say, is history. We started to blood Gordon towards the end of 1974, drafting him into the squad alongside a fellow youth-team player, Ian Anderson. It's fair to say Strachan went on to make the bigger impact, but it wasn't a given that he'd make it unless he could keep his attitude in check.

The majority were very supportive of me and of what we were trying to do. The centre-forward John Duncan went down to England within a couple of years of us taking over, and he was another of the exceptions. He clearly had his mind set on other things. He started treating matches like training games because his move was just round the corner. That's the way I saw it, anyway. He was sold to Spurs in the autumn of 1974, and the money, all £140,000 of it, was very useful to a club like Dundee. But we weren't under pressure from the board to sell players. The difference in Duncan's case was that he'd made it clear that he didn't want to be at Dens. In a situation like that, you're best to cut your losses, and the bonus in this particular case was that we were able to rake in a very healthy transfer fee.

Jocky Scott was also on the staff. He was an interesting character, and I have a wee chuckle to myself when I read now about Jocky the coach – the tough taskmaster, the disciplinarian. I didn't dislike Jocky at all, but he hated being given orders. It's a bit ironic that he went on to make a very good living in management from telling other people what to do!

We also had the wing-half Jim Steele, who was a very decent player. He was moved on to Southampton in an £80,000 transfer early in 1972. We'd not been long in the door, but it was too good to turn down and the wheels had already been in motion when John Prentice was still in charge. Leeds United had been keen at one stage, but it was the Saints who came good in the end. There'd been something of a tradition of shipping talent south of the border, with Alan Gilzean to Spurs and Ian Ure to Arsenal, as well as Charlie Cooke to Chelsea. The scouts kept returning to Dens and we got used to a steady stream of speculation surrounding our players. No bad thing, since they must have been doing something right. Iain Phillip was the next to go, snapped up by Crystal Palace before coming back for a second spell.

Some of the money that came in was reinvested in the side, with £20,000 spent on Wilson Hoggan from Falkirk. He was a speedy, two-footed midfielder who knew the way to goal, and the type of player Davie liked to build a team around. Thomson Allan, who had been freed by Hibs before being signed for Dundee by John Prentice, became a key player and proved a very talented goalkeeper for us, while Bobby Wilson was there too, one of a clutch of good players. Another, Mike Hewitt, had been with me at Queen's Park, so there was at least one familiar face when I reported for duty to take my first training session. The winger Duncan Lambie and defender Ronnie Selway were there too, and Bobby Robinson was in midfield.

The captain was Doug Houston, who proved to be a very sought-after player. We had our neighbours to contend with on that front, as Jim McLean had just taken over as manager at Dundee United. He had been assistant to John Prentice at Dens and in many eyes had been the obvious choice to take over when the time came for the manager to step aside, but the club's board obviously had other ideas and went for Davie instead. Whether that was his motivation I don't know, but he was persistent in his pursuit of Houston at around the time I joined the club. It was all good fun, nothing wrong with a bit of friendly rivalry or a spot of mischief-making. We politely declined those offers and Doug eventually got a move to what I'd consider bigger and better things.

He left at the end of the 1972–73 season, which was our first full campaign in charge and one we could be satisfied with. We finished two points better off than the year before, and it was good enough for fifth place again, level on points with Aberdeen in fourth and with only Hibs, Rangers and the champions, Celtic, ahead of us when it was all totalled up.

It was a typical Davie White team, with the emphasis on fast and fluent attacking football. He always put pace very high on his list of priorities when it came to choosing players to fit his system and loved to get his sides raiding forward at every opportunity. Not that the defensive side was neglected. We went through that entire season without being beaten at home, only drawing four of our games at Dens. It was excellent form, and Doug Houston won his move to Rangers on the back of it – adding an extra £50,000 to the kitty.

George Stewart, at centre-half, was another of the consistent performers, along with Bobby Wilson and Gordon Wallace. We still had John Duncan and Jocky Scott scoring the goals, and there was a good balance to that side.

If we'd had a bit of luck, we could have had a cup final to look forward to as well, having run Celtic close in both of the knockout competitions. We took them to a replay in the Scottish Cup semi-final when we held them to a 0–0 draw, but unfortunately we lost 3–0 in the rematch. It was a sore one, given that they'd also put us out of the League Cup at the quarter-final stage that season. It had been another replay after we'd ended locked at 3–3 after the two regulation legs of the tie. So near yet so far. It felt like our chance was gone, but we didn't realise what was around the corner.

It was the 1973–74 season, the one that would give me more satisfaction than any other I had as a coach. It kicked off as normal with the League Cup group games taking up the whole of August, with pools of four featuring home and away games against every side. We had a tough draw, with Hearts and Partick in with us and a couple of Tayside derbies against St Johnstone to contend with. Still, we fancied our chances of doing well. What we didn't expect was to go through the six group games unbeaten, having won all the home games and come away with draws from the matches at Tynecastle and Perth as well as a win at Firhill.

It teed us up for a second-round tie against Dunfermline, to be played over two legs, and we had the added distraction of European football to contend with, having won a place in the UEFA Cup. We tackled the Dutch side Twente Enschede in the first round of the competition. It was Davie's first game back at that level since the Górnik disaster with Rangers, but as usual he took it all in his stride, although there was no fairy-tale outcome and we were outclassed by the men from the Netherlands. We went out 7–3 on aggregate, but, given what was happening domestically, it might have been no bad thing.

We had two cracking ties against Dunfermline in the League Cup, winning 3–2 at East End Park and then drawing 2–2 at Dens to go through to the quarter-finals. The reward was another two-legged affair, this time against Clyde. We beat them with the

218

only goal of the game at Dens and held out for a 2–2 draw in the away game.

To reach the semi-final of the League Cup was an achievement in itself, but when we came out of the hat with Kilmarnock we began to sense we had a real chance of making the final. That would be something special if we could do it, and all of our energy went into making sure we did.

Attention to detail was one of Davie's best qualities. Davie had instigated specialised goalkeeping coaching as far back as his Clyde days, something that was unheard of elsewhere. He'd take the sessions himself, working the keepers hard, and it was just the type of detail that made him an exceptional manager. I can remember at Dundee when we were drawn to face Stranraer in the Scottish Cup, the manager ordered the groundsman at Dens to narrow the pitch to the exact dimensions of Stair Park, where we would travel to play the tie, so the squad could train on it and get used to the narrower park.

When it came to the League Cup semi-final, he gave Killie all the respect in the world. It worked. We did a really professional job on them and came through 1–0 to earn our place at the big table – and it was to be Celtic who were sitting on the other side.

Given they'd had something of an Indian sign over Dundee in cup competitions for years by that point, a lot of supporters must have looked at it as the worst possible outcome for us. Anyone but Celtic! Davie and I looked at it a bit differently. Yes, Celtic were on an incredible run of dominance – well on their way to nine in a row in the league by that point – but it didn't scare us. We didn't see them as unbeatable by any stretch of the imagination, but maybe that was just the old Rangers in us!

Besides, this was our big chance to prove that we had been treated roughly when it had ended at Ibrox. If we could take Dundee to Hampden and beat Celtic, it would vindicate everything we'd been trying to do.

And we did it. To go on and win against Celtic was just phenomenal. It was the cherry on top of what had been such a composed cup run.

The victory hinged on a tactical decision. The wind was strong that day and we set out our stall when we were against it, unashamedly negative. It was all about keeping them out at all costs in that first 45 minutes, and it worked a treat. The boys ran their socks off for us.

At the break, we shuffled things about, loaded up the front line and told them to miss out the midfield. We had players who were strong in the air, and we knew we could cause Celtic problems. It paid off beautifully. We never looked like losing, and in the end they were struggling to get hold of the ball.

A lot of people thought that for Davie it would have been about putting one over on Jock Stein, the man who in many ways had been the biggest obstacle to him staying at Rangers for far longer. But it wasn't like that, Celtic were there to be beaten for so many years, but there wasn't animosity. It was up to us and the rest of the teams to try to knock them off their perch, and we managed to do that in the final.

Besides, Davie had far bigger things on his mind. His wife was terribly ill. She was later diagnosed with multiple sclerosis and died at the age of 44. I think that put football well and truly in perspective for him.

While it might not have been important in the scheme of things, from a professional point of view there was no doubting the significance of the result. It proved that Davie had what it took to be a winner at the top level, and it also demonstrated that our Dundee side was one to be reckoned with. Winning league titles would always be difficult with a provincial side – not impossible, as the likes of Aberdeen would prove in the 1980s – but the cup competitions gave us a chance to show that on our day we could match even the Old Firm.

It gave the dark-blue half of the city a massive lift, and the celebrations were deserved. The final fell just ten days before Christmas, giving the Dens fans reason to start the party early.

In what proved to be a memorable season, we had some more drama to contend with in the months ahead. The Scottish Cup paired us with Aberdeen in the third round, our first game in that season's competition. It was a tough, tough fixture, but we were buoyed by our success in the League Cup and came through to win 2–0 up at Pittodrie. When the draw was made for the fourth round, I think it was written in the stars: Rangers v. Dundee. We were going back to Ibrox for a huge game.

Given that Celtic were looking odds-on for the championship and we'd already won the League Cup, it represented Jock Wallace's last chance of winning a trophy that season. Jock had stepped up to take over from Willie Waddell after the side's success in the European Cup-Winners' Cup in 1972, but there was no question that Waddell was still a major influence behind the scenes. That gave us a little extra motivation, to put it mildly.

I remember it like it was yesterday. For some reason, a clutch of the Scottish Cup ties were played on a Sunday, and ours was one of them. It was one of the first times there'd been Sunday football in Scotland, and it turned out not to be a day of rest for Rangers; we didn't give them a minute that day, we were at them from the kick-off.

We had done our homework as usual and looked at where we thought we could exploit their weaknesses. I'd noticed in the games I'd watched them play that John Greig was getting sucked further and further forward. He was going after wonder-goals, and I thought there was a gap we could exploit. It was the one time I told Jocky Scott not to bother about the team pattern or tracking back; I told him just to stay up there and wait for the ball to come to him. He did that, and sure enough we were able to ping it up to him whenever they came charging forward. Jocky would be there in a flash to get in behind. It all went to plan, or even better than we could have expected.

By the time the full-time whistle sounded, we were 3–0 ahead and absolutely cruising. We had hammered them; there were no two ways about it. I was called onto the park just before the game ended, and that made it all the sweeter because as I walked off I could see the faces of Waddell and the Ibrox directors and they were looking far from happy. I'm not ashamed to say he got the V-sign that day – it wasn't an anti-Rangers thing, it was anti one man, and that man was Willie Waddell. His team had been thrashed – and it was great. There's no way it made up for being turfed out of Ibrox all those years previously, but it did help with the healing process.

We went down to our old foes Celtic in the semi-final, losing 1–0 in a nervy game, but we could comfort ourselves with the fact that we already had a trophy on the mantelpiece.

In the league, we remained consistent, again taking fifth place. It was the fourth year on the trot the club had finished in the same spot, no mean feat given the number of quality players who had been lost over the years to bigger teams.

Jocky Scott was one of the next to go, leaving in the summer of 1975 when he was sold to Aberdeen. We got a £15,000 cheque as well as the services of Ian Purdie, who had been a Scotland Under-23 player at one point.

By then, my own time at Dundee was also at an end. From the very start, I'd told Davie that three years was the most I could give it, and when those three years were up I made the move to the Highlands.

It had been a long-standing ambition to set up a business on the west coast, one I'd harboured as far back as my days as a player with Rangers, when I first visited the area. Although I had enjoyed my spell at Dens Park, the time had come to make the break from football and start a new chapter in the family's life.

I'd applied for a grant to build a hotel at Gairloch, and I didn't know when that opportunity would come around again. We had the land if we wanted it and had the funding. It was a case of now or never in that respect. So we made the leap and moved on.

Davie needed a hard man beside him, and he didn't stay on too much longer after I'd gone. I can understand why people who didn't know him didn't necessarily rate him, but if you took the time to watch and listen, you soon realised he was ahead of his time in so many ways. In today's game, he'd be worth his weight in gold. It's just unfortunate that he wasn't given the chances he deserved when he was in his prime. You'd have had to have asked him yourself what he made of it all, but I wouldn't have blamed him for feeling mightily let down by the way his management career petered out while others with less nous and ability soldiered on for years and never seemed to find themselves out of work. It can be a strange game in that respect. Maybe he didn't keep in with the right people.

In the summer of 1976, Dundee dropped out of the Premier Division, with the relegation battle going right to the wire. It was the first season of the league's existence in its ten-team guise, and there was a lot of hype surrounding it. While it created excitement because it was new, the format with fewer teams removed a safety blanket, and unfortunately it was my old club that suffered.

It came down to a double-header against Motherwell at the end of the season, with a 1–1 draw in the first game giving hope before a 1–0 win in the next game. It all counted for nothing, though, with Dundee United taking an unexpected point on the final day of the season against Rangers to finish level on points with their city neighbours but stay up by virtue of a better goal difference. Mr McLean at Tannadice must have enjoyed that, in the spirit of rivalry we had with them.

I remember in 1976, after Dundee had been relegated, Davie had a real pop at the players in the media and questioned their integrity. Bearing in mind they were top of the First Division and on course for a return to the Premier Division at that point, it hinted that all was not well. Dundee was a well-supported club, and that brought its own pressures. If the team didn't perform, you felt the paying public were being cheated. Davie never wanted to see that happening and wouldn't be shy of reminding the squad of their responsibilities on that front. He took his own job seriously and wanted everyone to do the same, understandably. He was also a worker and demanded the same sort of ethic from those on his staff, something I'd always admired in the man.

When the manager departed in 1977, they didn't have to look far for his successor. Tommy Gemmell, who had been part of the playing staff for a good four years, was the man they chose. He was in his early 30s, but, as one of the Lisbon Lions, was a big-name appointment for a club keen to return to former glories. He had been a major signing when he arrived in 1973, released by Nottingham Forest. Davie saw him as a solid, experienced player to add to the mix. It turned out he would also be his successor in the manager's office, but Tommy would struggle to repeat the cup-winning exploits of the man from whom he took over.

Just as I left Queen's Park with fantastic memories, I look back on Dundee with great fondness. When we won the cup, it was mission accomplished and I could retire from football content, with another win under my belt and with the ghosts of the Rangers experience well and truly exorcised.

25

MACKENZIE COUNTRY

I HAVE GONE THROUGH MY life with headlines screaming 'Davis this' and 'Davis that'; the front cover of this book has 'Davis' emblazoned across it; the sign at the bottom of my driveway is etched with 'Davis'. In fact, though, my name shouldn't be Harold Davis at all: my bloodline is Mackenzie.

My father was Angus Mackenzie, my mother Catherine McQueen Kirk, so there's not a Davis among us, technically speaking. The name came from the fact that my grandmother on my father's side had remarried and changed her name to Davis. Gran was a very dominant woman, and my father took on the Davis name too. I don't think he would have had too much choice in the matter! He'd have done what his mother told him and kept in her good books, like all good sons would.

Given my clan roots, it's perhaps fitting that when it came to putting down permanent roots it was right here in the heart of Mackenzie country that we chose to settle.

I first visited the West Highlands when I went north on a little expedition in 1959. I stumbled upon the fabulous Fionn Loch and sampled the rugged beauty of Loch na h-Oidhche and the almost eerie peace of Loch Bad a Chreamh.

Angling had been a passion since I was a wee boy, but it was while I was with Rangers that I began to get really wrapped up in it. I had a little caravan that I'd hitch to the back of the car, and I'd head into the hills when I had a couple of days off, setting out from our home near Ibrox and pointing the car in the direction of one of my favourite spots.

Mind you, it wasn't always straightforward. Where we lived on Harrison Drive, virtually at the back door of Ibrox, was a wee dead end, and lots of kids would gather and play football up and down the street. When I came out to head for the hills, they'd all crowd round and have a laugh and a joke. One day, as normal, I shooed them away and drove off along my way. I was heading for a little salmon river out west, going through the Clyde Tunnel on my way. At the time, there were repairs going on at the tunnel, with a big drop between the road heading in and the one coming out the other direction.

I looked in my mirror as I headed down into the tunnel – and quickly realised that the caravan that should have been reflected back at me was nowhere to be seen. Then, in an instant, I saw it come into view and hurtle towards me on its jockey wheel. I put my foot on the accelerator to try to get clear, or at least cushion the impact, and sure enough it came thumping into the back of the car and caused havoc at the tunnel entrance. With a bit of help from security, who had been watching the whole carry-on through their camera system, a recovery truck was with me within 30 seconds. They were able to get me patched up and off on my way again before the police could get involved; they had access to the CCTV footage, after all. My rescuer said, 'They wouldn't book you anyway.' Maybe he was right!

Those little trips with the caravan on the back were a great release. When you were in Glasgow, there would be well-wishers on every corner, wanting to stop for a chat. To get away from it all was nice every now and again.

I think that's why I enjoyed the freedom of the social side of football: we were all in the same boat. Whether it was playing golf with the boys or getting away to the hills, I had some great company through the clubs I was involved with.

The golf could get quite competitive, mind you, with matches between the football clubs organised from time to time. I can remember Rangers coming out on top at Crow Wood in one of those, with a certain Craig Brown helping us on our way to victory, along with Bobby Shearer, Johnny Hubbard and the late, great Bill Paterson.

Bill was a dear friend of mine and we liked nothing better than getting away for a spot of fishing and leaving the day job behind for a few hours. Jock Macdonald was another football man who became a great friend through the fishing. It was Jock, who died in 2008, who was the driving force behind the creation of Inverness Caledonian Thistle, and his family can be proud of his legacy to the game and proud of a great man.

I loved to head for the Highlands and Islands, where I've found some marvellous spots along the coast. I've been to South Uist every year for 40 years fishing and love it over there. It was one of my early discoveries during my searches for the best places to cast.

One of those expeditions took me to Wester Ross, and it was when I made my second trip, a year down the line, that I sat on a hillside and made a big decision. It was, quite simply, the best fishing I'd ever experienced, and I had fallen in love with the area in a heartbeat. From then on, I returned year in and year out, and I knew one day I'd call it home. It was a question of waiting for the right opportunity.

As it happened, the right opportunity never seemed to present itself. After leaving Rangers, I wound up back in football with Dundee and, although I was enjoying my work, it came to the point where it was time to look at the bigger picture, and time for a clean break.

I made up my mind to leave it all behind and head for the Highlands, start a new life in Gairloch, a place that already felt like home. Dundee tried to persuade me to stay – I can remember sitting with the chairman on the team bus with him desperately bending my ear – but my mind was made up.

It was a huge gamble, moving away from a good job in the game I loved and also leaving behind the poultry-farming business in Fife. We also left behind family and friends, setting off on our adventure.

We invested in a patch of ground just outside Gairloch and set about building ourselves a hotel, the business that was going to support our escape to the country. The plot was about eight feet deep in sloppy peat, so we had to excavate the whole site and lift out what we could before starting from there and laying the foundations of what would become the Creag Mor Hotel.

What I hadn't bargained on was a shortage of labour in the north, with all of the local builders tied up on projects and not available to start when we needed them. Instead, I had to rely on workers coming up from Glasgow – far from ideal but the best I could do to get the project off the ground and try to stick to our schedule.

It seemed to be coming along fine until one day I went up to the roof to inspect the work they were doing on the felting. Now, I'm no builder, but I know a botched job when I see one, and this was a disaster in full flow. It didn't help that the foreman was wearing Hush Puppies. I'm not sure he'd seen a building site before, let alone run one.

It went from bad to worse when I went downstairs and caught two of his finest operatives in action attempting to plaster one of the rooms. I was watching through the window in utter disbelief as one of these characters, hands on hips, watched the other as he basically threw plaster at the walls. I could hear the observer shouting, 'Hey, Jimmy, you've missed again,' as this hit and, more often than not, miss process carried on. It would have been funny if it wasn't our money being thrown up against the wall. I left when one of them lay down on the floor, gazing up, trying to spot the bits that hadn't been covered. It would have been a shorter process to find the parts that had been, mind you.

That was the final straw. I sacked the lot of them. I had to get another batch up from Glasgow and this time they were much better, aside from going round every room pointing out the jobs that hadn't been done right and suggesting ways of 'improving' some of the jobs that had already been carried out.

Once we overcame those hurdles, we opened up and got into the swing of life as hoteliers. Business was good, even if the hospitality trade did have its moments. We were a quiet country pub, but I still found myself having to disarm one of the customers as he threatened to go mad with a knife. Nothing like the quiet life!

To be fair, those types of incidents were very few and far between. We had wonderfully loyal regulars and guests who would come back again and again to stay at the hotel. Andy Menzies, a dear friend from Glasgow, had been my fishing companion for years and became a welcome visitor.

Mind you, it was hard work, and we soon discovered that we were wrong if we thought we'd be taking it easy after moving north. We worked hard, but it was rewarding and another string to our bows. Having the hotel was a way of surviving, as I never made enough at the game of football to save a penny.

We moved up as a family, together with our son Alan, and settled into a new life in the Highlands. Alan was born in Glasgow and returned to his home city through his work, still being settled there to this day.

He found a niche for himself in the world of classical music, as manager of the BBC Scottish Symphony Orchestra and, a little like myself, travelled the world in his role. Wherever they went, they would stay true to their roots, and one of the highlights for Alan was a performance in China when, after going through the usual repertoire of classical pieces, the orchestra returned for an encore with a selection of Scottish tunes. By all accounts, it brought the house down. Just like the Rangers tour to the USSR all those years ago, Alan's adventure in China was one of his more testing assignments – but he persevered, and the show did indeed go on. It's a long way from spending warm summer days in the hills around Gairloch to taking an orchestra to Tiananmen Square.

Vi and I are proud of everything he's done and now, back in Glasgow, he's enjoying a well-earned retirement. Not that he's taking it easy by any stretch of the imagination, with a project to become fluent in German well under way.

By the time we moved north, Vi and I had been married nearly 20 years, our wedding having taken place in Perth in March 1957. Now we are close to our diamond anniversary and looking forward to many more happy years together. It's the best team I've been involved with in my life.

After finding our feet in the hotel trade, we tried to make sure we had some time spare. We became enthusiastic members of Gairloch Golf Club, and still are. Vi likes to get out as often as she can for a round, although I'm playing less nowadays. We used to like to get away for a bit of winter sun in the off-season, heading for the golf courses in Portugal or Florida whenever we could.

It wasn't all leisurely breaks, mind you. That period wasn't without its drama. Having survived what the Chinese and Koreans could throw at me, I was lucky to pull through again after a potentially troublesome event far closer to home.

Vi and I were driving down past Oban on the Dalmally-to-Inveraray road, near Port Sonachan, with not a care in the world when we were involved in a terrifying accident. A car in front of me clipped the verge and careered across the road, crashing into a livestock truck. As the truck, laden with sheep, swerved to try to avoid the car, it toppled and we got embroiled in the crash. The truck tipped over onto our car, crushing it like a tin can. Vi was able to scramble clear and was taken to hospital by ambulance, suffering from whiplash. I was trapped and had to be cut out of the wreckage before being flown to hospital in Oban by helicopter, in excruciating pain.

The fact that they had scrambled an air ambulance hints at how seriously they were treating it, but they didn't realise at that point how critical my condition was. It wasn't until a very alert doctor realised it was more serious than most had thought that the extent of the injuries became clear. I had an X-ray and it became apparent that I'd broken my neck. Cue an emergency dash to the Royal Alexandra Hospital in Paisley, where I received specialist treatment and was eventually able to get out of my hospital bed and back on my feet. Just like the good old days.

I ended up wearing a big metal brace, screwed onto my head, to stabilise the area and allow me to recover. I had to eat and sleep in the thing. It wasn't pretty, but it was effective. Touch wood, I've never been bothered by those injuries since, and I'm just glad the break was spotted when it was. As with any spinal injury, if it had been left untreated the consequences could have been severe.

It's terrifying to look at the pictures of what was left of the car at the end of it: just a lump of twisted metal. It was a Toyota, but you'd be hard-pressed to tell that from looking at the photos! That's what a few tonnes of Scania can do.

Still, we came through that relatively unscathed and continued along in the hotel trade until it came time to retire from the business in the 1990s. We decided not to decamp too far. We bought a house overlooking the water and the village, tucked away high on the hillside and with wonderful views out towards Gairloch and beyond.

We have a fantastic spot and are surrounded by nature at its very best. We have a couple of pine martens who come calling at the patio doors each day, looking for the food and biscuits that we keep specially for them. It's a mix of bread and jam that they like. The previous owner of the house used to feed them and it's a ritual we're happy to stick to. They've become tame and one will even hop into the house to see us, given half a chance. Then there's my coal tits, who come calling later in the day for their feeding session. Vi says I'm like the Birdman of Gairloch, with these little fellows happy to nibble away on food from my hand. They come circling around the front window at the same time each day and know we'll look out for them.

While I love the birds and the wildlife, it's the fishing that remains my biggest passion. I've got a table at the big window at the front of the house, looking out towards the water, and can sit for hours tying flies. I've had some success with them, too, and I've developed a bit of a following for some of the designs. Whenever I go out on a trip, I'm sure to take my toothbrush with me to brush the hackles on my flies. That's dedication for you.

I'm happiest when I'm outdoors, though, down by the water. We're very fortunate in this part of the world to have very accommodating landowners, who support the angling community and do their very best to find that fine line between conservation and access for all.

Within a short hop from home, there are some incredible spots, and I have my own Argo Cat all-terrain vehicle for getting around the countryside and reaching even the most remote areas. It comes in particularly handy when we have guests staying for the fishing, which has become something of a sideline for Vi and me. I say for us, but in fact we do it for charity – one particular charity.

I've been a long-time supporter of Erskine, the veterans' trust. As a patron, I do whatever I can to help with the fund-raising efforts, and I travel the length and breadth of the country attending functions and events in the name of the charity. I've contributed a few auction lots over the year, including the blazer from the run to the 1961 European Cup-Winners' Cup final. That pulled in £2,500.

A few years back, we hit upon the idea of offering fishing trips, with anglers making a donation to Erskine. It has really blossomed, and we have people who come back year after year. I have to be careful, though, because we could end up busier in retirement than we were when we had the hotel going full tilt. We do as much as we can, but I like to make sure I keep a little bit of time aside for my own fishing. It's still a wonderful release to get out in the open and land a catch, with my record of a 29.5-lb salmon on the River Tay to be beaten, and plenty of trout out there, too. My great friend Roddy Mackenzie keeps me company and shares my love of the land.

Together with my fellow Wester Ross angling enthusiasts Stan Frost and Les Lamb, I wrote a book on fishing in the Gairloch area a few years back, and it was very well received. Hopefully, it has given a few people some pointers on the best places to head for and the readers got a feel for the enthusiasm we have for the area.

I'm just as enthusiastic about taking guests out and either teaching them to fish or helping the more experienced anglers unlock some of the hidden secrets of this part of the world. The fact that Erskine benefits is, of course, a huge bonus.

The charity has been in existence since 1916, supporting servicemen and women ever since then. It is as relevant today as it was back then, with help offered to veterans as well as the latest recruits.

There's a fantastic bond between Erskine and Rangers on many levels, from the club welcoming soldiers and veterans to Ibrox for games to the massive fund-raising effort that has taken place in recent years in the club's name.

The Rangers Supporters Erskine Appeal, which I am always delighted to support, has far exceeded everyone's expectations. What started in 2007 with the humble aim of raising £1,000 has mushroomed to the extent that in 2011 a massive £170,000 was pulled in. That took the running total past the £350,000 mark and represents a huge help to those charged with pushing a wonderful charity forward and extending its reach.

It costs more than £20,000 a day to keep up the good work, so every penny counts. That money goes towards providing everything from residential care to physiotherapy and other medical services. I know all too well the pitfalls of service, and for there to be such a professional and well-run safety net back at home is a huge reassurance not only for those who served their country long ago but also for those heading for Afghanistan and other foreign climes now.

There are Erskine care homes in Edinburgh, Anniesland, Bishopton and Erskine, as well as partnership homes in Aberdeen, Inverness, Perth, Dundee and Dumfries. It's an impressive network and deserves all of our support.

That's why Vi and I are happy to do whatever we're asked. Whether it's signing prints or speaking at dinners, I'm ready and willing to do whatever is required. I'm far from alone in that respect, with an incredibly dedicated band of volunteers up and down the land pulling together an amazing programme of events and getting support from many former Rangers players in the process.

We're kept busy and rack up the miles, but we wouldn't have it any other way. After all the adventures we've been through together, I think it's fair to say the quiet life was never for us!

26

ON REFLECTION

THREE OR FOUR YEARS AGO, I had a call out of the blue. A man on the other end told me his name and explained he had served in Korea with me. I recognised the name and could picture his face in a flash, conjuring up memories of those days back on the line.

We talked about the night I was shot. It turned out he had been in gun pit No. 1 and was one of the men I was looking after that night. He could remember as vividly as I could how high the tensions were running and how nervous everyone was. Stomachs were in knots. It was that type of evening where it felt like something would go wrong.

Talking to him brought it all flooding back and, unexpected as it was, it was good to talk to someone who had been through it and get a different perspective on what was going on around us.

Then came the bit I hadn't been expecting. My man went on to apologise, explaining that he thought it was him who had shot me. As confessions go, that one was right up there with the best of them.

He was genuine, he was full of remorse and he was heartfelt in what he said. Just as I remembered it, he spoke of the confusion that enveloped the position. Guns were going off all over the place, and he was convinced that his bullets had taken me down.

He had gone through life blaming himself and had finally tracked me down and plucked up the courage to confront the issue head-on. It took guts for him to go through with it. I can imagine it must have been bouncing around in his head for years up to that point.

I've no idea what sort of reaction he was anticipating, but all I could do was reassure him that he would never know for sure if he had hit me. Even if he had, and I doubt it very much, in those circumstances there's no way you could apportion blame. They were shooting at us, we were shooting at them – I was the unfortunate one stuck in the middle of it all.

Perhaps he had thought I'd spent all these years mulling it over myself, wondering who had shot me ... what they looked like, what they'd been thinking when they pulled the trigger, whether they knew the pain they'd caused. In truth, none of those things had entered my mind. I was far too busy trying to recover as best I could to worry about any of that.

Besides, we were soldiers in the middle of a bloody and brutal war. I carried a gun, the same as everyone else, and fired it in anger. If you're prepared to give it, you have to be prepared to take it. The only problem is that in that environment the consequences are a little more severe than when you're in a squabble in the school playground. The principle's the same, though.

I'm sure my man was worried that he'd be dredging up painful memories, but he needn't have troubled himself. I'm reminded every day of what happened to me; my body tells the story.

My bladder shrunk with all the scar tissue from the operations, and I have to judge how many toilets there are along the way for every journey. All these little quirks and routines have been woven into my life – I daren't stop them. The bladder sometimes feels like it is going to stop altogether, but by remembering to do the right things I can make sure I stay healthy.

Doing that virtually rules my life. I'm thinking about it all the time. I've to eat the right things. Every morning, I have porridge and six heaped soupspoons of bran, raw bran. I've found I have to live my life a different way, and I would say it has helped me in the long run, so I'm not complaining.

People look at what I went on to do, the long career I had in sport, and think I must have been OK. After all, if I was fit enough to run around kicking people on a football pitch, I must have been fine. Well, not quite. There were times when I would have to run off the pitch in the middle of a game to go to the toilet. Those were the days before substitutes, so it wasn't as though they could send on a replacement. I'd blame it on cramp. Nobody ever questioned it, so I didn't have too much explaining to do.

I would experience difficulties in all sorts of different circumstances; there was always something round the corner. For example, when we went on foreign trips the travelling could be a problem ... not to mention the facilities. The stand-up toilets in Eastern Europe were an education.

Those are the kinds of problems I've faced throughout my life, but I'm well aware that there may be others waiting to come back and bite me as a result of the trauma my body went through back then.

Still, I'm a greater believer in 'what will be will be'. Even when things were at their worst and it was touch and go, I never found myself praying to any god. I'm not a religious person at all. What I would say is that I believe very much in the principles of the church, and I have nothing against churchgoers. I just don't want to be one of them. I admire a lot of church people but can't help but wonder why, if there's a god, so many nice people, so many children, end up dead? It is all up to the individual, but I never even in my darkest hour turned to God.

Instead, I've always preferred to take what's coming my way, and that won't change in the years ahead. I'll keep doing the right things and live well, trusting that will see me right. After all, why change the habit of a lifetime?

Whatever problems I face now or in later life, the bottom line is I survived. My fellow veterans and I are grateful for that, and in recent years I've come to appreciate more and more that common bond we share. The 60th anniversary celebrations of the Battle of the Hook in 2012 brought us back together as part of the Black Watch family for a special reunion, and it's events like that which rekindle the memories and evoke the old emotions once more.

Researching aspects of this book has also put me back in touch with the regiment, particularly the incredibly helpful people at the Black Watch Museum in Perth, and others who have written about their experiences in the war. It has been a thought-provoking process.

The regret is that the conflict has become known as 'the Forgotten War'. Because it was a United Nations force we were part of, dominated by the Americans, in numbers at least, it wasn't viewed as a 'British' war as such. That means the names of the 1,090 men who died have, in many cases, not been given the prominence they deserve. There are memorials dedicated to victims of the war in Glasgow and Perth, but the largest permanent tribute is at Witchcraig, near Bathgate. There is a site there dedicated to the conflict – complete with Korean firs and a pavilion modelled on a traditional Korean house – where all of the soldiers killed in action are listed. It opened more than a decade ago, and it is nice to think that there's a permanent and lasting memorial to the many men who lost their lives on those hills and fields around the dreaded Hook.

ON REFLECTION

More than any structure or plaque, the important thing is to make sure that memories of what was a brutal and bloody war are preserved for future generations. The men who made the ultimate sacrifice deserve to be remembered, and the lessons of Korea are there for all to see.

ON REFLECTION

More than any structure or plaque, the important thing is to make sure that memories of what was a brutal and bloody war are preserved for future generations. The men who made the ultimate sacrifice deserve to be remembered, and the lessons of Korea are there for all to see.